THE ENCHANTED SUITCASE

A WINDOW ONTO MY GERMAN FATHER'S WORLD WAR II LIFE

HELGA WARREN

Black Rose Writing | Texas

©2023 by Helga Warren
All rights reserved. No part of this book may be reproduced, stored in a retrieval system or transmitted in any form or by any means without the prior written permission of the publishers, except by a reviewer who may quote brief passages in a review to be printed in a newspaper, magazine or journal.

The author grants the final approval for this literary material.

First printing

Some names and identifying details have been changed to protect the privacy of individuals.

ISBN: 978-1-68513-095-4
PUBLISHED BY BLACK ROSE WRITING
www.blackrosewriting.com

Printed in the United States of America
Suggested Retail Price (SRP) $21.95

The Enchanted Suitcase is printed in Sabon

*As a planet-friendly publisher, Black Rose Writing does its best to eliminate unnecessary waste to reduce paper usage and energy costs, while never compromising the reading experience. As a result, the final word count vs. page count may not meet common expectations.

Cover design by Cliff Warren
German POW cover photo courtesy of the Aliceville Museum

To Bea,
Helga Warren ♡

For Marcello and Adalie

ACKNOWLEDGEMENTS

I wish to thank Reagan Rothe sincerely and the entire team at Black Rose Writing, including reader Robert Favarato, for taking a chance on me.

I also owe an incalculable debt to John Gillum, director of the Aliceville Museum and German POW Exhibit, and to Ruth Beaumont Cook, author of the definitive history of the town of Aliceville, Alabama and the POW Camp, *Guests Behind the Barbed Wire: German POWs in America: A True Story of Hope and Friendship,* for their continued insightful support, encouragement, advice and all-around helpfulness. Ruth, in particular, freely offered her expert editorial advice, which helped make my manuscript so much better.

To Mimi Schwartz, noted Princeton, NJ author and professor, for suggesting that I incorporate my father's books in a memoir of my own. To Betty Lies, talented memoir-writing instructor at the Princeton Senior Resource Center, for getting me started and pointing out that my suitcase was truly "enchanted".

To my good friend and prolific author Shari Randall for her expert help in demystifying the publishing industry for me and pointing out the universality of my father's soldier life, as well as her unfailing good humor.

To my cousin Peter's wife, Martine Boyer-Weinmann, for sharing her brilliant intellect with me. She wrote a book about my mother in French, which is being published in France, and we are in continuous contact—to my immense benefit.

I wish to thank my sister, Marie Schwartz, for encouraging and supporting me in writing about our parents. I would also like to thank my son Cliff Warren for the gift of his hugely creative cover design and constant enthusiasm, as well as his wife Lola Catero, for her example of inspiring feminism and respect for all peoples. My daughter Macy Graham is the kindest person and most devoted daughter I know. Her husband Brendan's compassion and empathy positively impact everyone who comes in contact with him.

Deepest gratitude to my wonderful husband Harry Warren, without whom none of this would have been possible. He is overwhelmingly responsible for the happy adult life I have been privileged enough to lead, and I would be nowhere without his love and support.

And last of all, profound gratitude to my parents, Karlheinz Stoess and Irene Misslbeck Stoess, for inspiring me both then and now with the interesting lives they led.

THE ENCHANTED
SUITCASE

PART I: DISCOVERING

PART II: DECODING

PART III: DOCUMENTING

PART 1: DISCOVERING

There was a suitcase in my basement. It was quite nondescript, nothing special, one of those hard-sided Samsonite suitcases with the streamlined locks from the pre-wheeled-suitcase era. You would probably never give it a second glance, and I had paid little attention to it. It had rested there, black, scratched and undisturbed at the bottom of a vast pile of boxes, for several decades. What was special about it was what it contained: all that remained of my father's papers and possessions after he died in 1986, over 35 years ago, from Non-Hodgkin lymphoma at age 66.

My mother had left the suitcase in my basement in Springfield, Virginia years ago for safekeeping, when in 1996 she suddenly moved back to Europe (at a still energetic age 75). One quiet afternoon, I decided it was finally time to open the suitcase. It was 2017, the year I turned 60. My two children were grownups. I had retired from teaching German. I finally had some time to myself, and it was then that I started sorting through and reflecting on the fascinating details of my father's younger life.

A basic biography would start this way: Born Karlheinz Rudolf Stöss on July 1, 1920, he emigrated to the United States from Germany in 1951, later "Americanizing" his name to Karl H. R. Stoess. During World War II, he served as a *Feldwebel* (technical sergeant) in the *Luftwaffe* (German air force) and was captured in Normandy shortly after D-Day. While behind barbed wire in Alabama as a prisoner of war, he served as a camp interpreter because of his excellent English. He worked closely with and became friends with American officer Robert "Bob" Hahnen of Minnesota, who later acted as his immigration sponsor.

After settling in the Washington, DC area in 1951, Karlheinz took night classes at George Washington University Law School and eventually became a patent attorney. His sister and mother had preceded him to the United States after his sister's marriage to an American army officer. Karlheinz had met my mother at Erlangen University in Germany after the war; subsequently she studied in Canada and they had been corresponding regularly. He sent for her in 1953 so that they could marry and begin a new life together in America. Unlike many of their compatriots who wanted nothing more than to fit into American society in a German-hostile post-war era, my parents persisted in speaking German to each other and later to my sister and me. I can't say that they ever assimilated.

• • •

Feldwebel Karlheinz Rudolf Stoess, undated

The suitcase was full of identification cards, photographs, diplomas, expired passports and elementary school report cards covered with spidery *Kurrent*, Old German handwriting that I didn't know how to read. A fake leather wallet had melted and disintegrated over some documents, making a sticky mess. There was a box of letters from my father to my mother that she had carefully saved, tied with a yellow ribbon. I do not know what he did with her letters to him. There were photos of his various previous girlfriends, catalogued into individual envelopes with their names written on the front in my mother's handwriting. There was a stack of letters to a woman who was not my mother. The suitcase, assembled by my mother after my father's death, was all that remained of his possessions.

A tattered envelope contained a pile of yellowed pages with faint handwriting on them. Flipping them over, I saw they were American Army requisition forms from World War II. My father had used the backs of the forms to write on. I realized that this must be one of the two memoirs my father had written during and after the war. My sister had the other one, a neatly handwritten, bound book with a green cover that she had had since my father's death. I only faintly remembered it and had never looked inside.

The biggest surprise of all was a folder of letters stamped "CENSORED" from the German POW camp in Aliceville, Alabama, where my father was a prisoner of war for about two years. Later I was to learn that there were German POW camps all over the United States, especially in the South, even in Virginia, where I lived. The young American men marched off to war and there was no one to harvest the crops or do the farm work except for the German prisoners, of whom there were plenty: over 400,000 in all. My father had always talked favorably about Alabama and the kind farmers who put out lavish lunchtime spreads of barbequed ribs and biscuits. Food was good and plentiful in the POW camp, and he said it was the only time during the war that he had enough to eat.

I knew the British had captured Karlheinz in a bunker on the Normandy coast a few days after D-Day, on Sword Beach. They had transferred these prisoners (known as "British-owned") to the Americans because the British barely had enough food or housing for themselves, much less German prisoners.

• • •

The letters with the earliest dates on them were to the woman who was not my mother. I pieced together that she was not a girlfriend, but a young lady he had met in passing when he was 17 and she was 15, by the name of Editha Sobbe. He seemed to have known her parents and had dined with the family at least once, which is when he met Editha. There was no evidence of a romantic connection in the letters.

He wrote his letters to Editha from the various countries where he was stationed, and they confirmed what I had always been told: that my father had never seen combat—his great intelligence and aptitude for learning had spared him the heat of battle. Instead, he attended officer training school, completing one course of study after another on his way to promotion to officer. He was always to remain an officer candidate and never to receive full promotion, because of his capture and the subsequent end of the war. From the letters, I could put together a comprehensive timeline of where he had been and when. Previously, I had had only bits and pieces of information that now fit together into a coherent whole.

It might help to clarify the regular German *Wehrmacht* (not SS/Nazi) military ranks and their US Army equivalents, which will be of importance for the rest of this narrative:

German Military Ranks and their US Equivalents
Soldat, Schütze, Grenadier - Private
Oberschütze - Private 1st class
Gefreiter - Acting corporal

Obergefreiter - Corporal

Fahnenjunker - Unteroffizier OA - Officer aspirant/candidate

Unteroffizier - Sergeant

Unterfeldwebel - Staff sergeant

Feldwebel - Technical sergeant

Fähnrich - NCO officer candidate, equivalent in rank to *Feldwebel*

Oberfeldwebel - Master sergeant

Hauptfeldwebel - Senior NCO (no exact US Army equivalent rank)

Stabsfeldwebel - Sergeant major

Leutnant - Second lieutenant

Oberleutnant - First lieutenant

Hauptmann/Rittmeister - Captain

Major - Major

Oberstleutnant - Lieutenant colonel

Oberst - Colonel

General - General

• • •

Following is a chronology of the major events in Karlheinz's life that I reconstructed from the papers that were in the suitcase, as well as that part of his trajectory during the war, as documented by the letters to Editha Sobbe. This also serves as scaffolding for what follows in his writings:

KARLHEINZ STOESS TIMELINE (1920-1986)

July 1, 1920

Born Lutheran in Dresden, Germany to Bernhard Rudolf Stöss (known as Rudolf) and Elisabeth Elsa Günther Stöss (known as Else).

1926-1939

Attended the *Dietrich-Eckart-Schule*, municipal school in Dresden. Graduated 1939 from the *Oberrealschule Dresden-Johannstadt*, with the German high school *Abitur* degree.

1940

Unpaid labor service at a bank, the *Beamtenbank Dresden*, from January 1 to April 11, 1940.

KARLHEINZ STOESS DURING WORLD WAR II (1939-1946)

This part of the chronology came from Karlheinz Stoess's letters to Editha Sobbe (later Editha Finzel). He met her around Easter of 1938 when he was still 17 and she was 15. He started writing to her in October 1939, when he was 19 and she was 17. She later returned to him the letters he had written to her, and they remained good friends throughout the subsequent decades.

Hitler invaded Poland on September 1, 1939. This was the official beginning of World War II.

October-December 1939 (19 years old)—Poland
Member of a *Baubattailon* (Construction Brigade), probably under the auspices of the *RAD* (*Reichsarbeitsdienst*), a compulsory labor service for adolescent males during the Third Reich.

December 1939 (19 years old)—Returned to his home in Dresden, Germany (Teutoburgerstrasse 1)
Released from the compulsory labor service.

January 1940-December 1941 (19-21 years old)—Laon, France
Drafted into the *Wehrmacht* (German army); served as a Teletype operator.

January 1942 (21 years old)—Brussels, Belgium
Member of the *Abteilungsstab* (battalion headquarters).
Completed two courses of military study during this time.

July 1, 1942 (his 22ⁿᵈ birthday)—Brussels, Belgium
Promoted to *Unteroffizier* (Non-Commissioned Officer, sergeant)
after having passed his first six-week course, *Unteroffizier-Anwärter-Lehrgang* (NCO-candidate course of study).

Combat Duty in Belgium, July 1942

August 1, 1942 (22 years old)—Brussels, Belgium
Promoted to *Kriegsoffizier-Bewerber* (lieutenant candidate) after having passed his second six-week course, *Kriegsoffizier-Vorauswahllehrgang* (aspiring lieutenant pre-selection course of study).

Mid-October 1942 (22 years old)—Halle, Germany
Started another course of study to advance to officer status, *Offizierslehrgang* (officer course of study).

December 18, 1942-January 5, 1943 (22 years old)—Dresden
Christmas vacation at home with his family.

January 1943 (22 years old)—Luc-sur-Mer, France
Sent to the Normandy coast in France (near Caen) to work in "secret" barracks, a bunker, and a radar station. He manned *Geräte* (radar devices) intended to monitor enemy aircraft.

February 25, 1943 (22 years old)
His brother Siegfried died at the Russian front in Czarków, Russia at age 21. He was an *SS-Rottenführer* (Nazi squad leader—highest SS enlisted rank).

March 1943-April 1943 (22 years old)—Arnhem, Holland
Sent to Holland to complete a course of study/apprenticeship for tracking enemy aircraft at night.

April 1943 (22 years old)—Arnhem, Holland
Promoted to *Feldwebel* (technical sergeant), the highest rank he achieved in the German *Wehrmacht*.

May 1943 (22 years old)—Dresden, Germany
Vacation in Dresden at home with his family after passing through Amsterdam, Brussels and Paris, once his training in Holland was complete, and he had returned to France. Visited Leipzig and Köln on his way back to France from Dresden.

End of May 1943 (22 years old)—Luc-sur-Mer, France
Returned to the bunker on the Normandy coast and transferred to Saint-Malo, France, from where he would ship out to the Isle of Guernsey in June 1943. He was now an NCO in the *Luftwaffe* (German air force).

July 1943 (23 years old)—Isle of Guernsey ("States of Guernsey")
Rank was that of *OA* or *Offizier Anwärter* (officer candidate); worked in a *Flugmeldemaßkompanie* (flight reporting company/platoon).

August 1943 (23 years old)—Dresden-Klotzsche, Germany
Sent to Germany for flight reporting training for five weeks; lived at home during this time.

October 1943 (23 years old)—Paris, France
Sent to Paris via Caen, after a brief stop in Bayeux where he was supposed to be posted. This change in orders was an unexpected and welcome surprise. In Paris, his assignment was to the *Flugwachkommando Paris* or *"Fluko Paris"* (Paris Flight Surveillance Command) to transmit *Luftlagereportagen* (status reports on flights). His assignment there was for only one month and this is where he met Michi, the subject of his first memoir, *Das Buch Michi*, (*The Book of Michi*).

Mid-November 1943 (23 years old)—Dresden, Germany
Back at home on vacation.

End of November 1943 (23 years old)—Luc-sur-Mer, France
Back in the bunker in France.

January-March 1944 (23 years old)—Luc-sur-Mer, France
The Germans feared an Allied Invasion, and there had already been several bombings of Berlin.

Normandy, France, 1944

April 1944 (23 years old)—Luc-sur-Mer, France
Worked in the capacity of *Zugführer* (platoon leader).

May 1944 (23 years old)—Dresden, Germany
Back on vacation in Dresden.

May 24, 1944 (23 years old)
The date of the last letter he wrote to Editha Sobbe. An empty
envelope from a letter she wrote him in reply (sent to Paris) had
been returned to her, postmarked June 6, 1944 (D-Day). He was
captured eight days later by the British and sent to a German
prisoner of war camp in Aliceville, Alabama after a brief sojourn
in England. The empty envelope is among his papers. He hand-

wrote his first novel (*Das Buch Michi*) while he was a POW at Camp Aliceville and it was bound in the prison bookbindery.

November 20, 1944 (24 years old)
His father, Rudolf Stöss, died of tuberculosis (referred to as pleurisy) at age 50 in a German sanatorium.

Prisoner Nr. 31G-5060, Company Nr. 20,
Aliceville German POW Camp, Aliceville, Alabama, 1944

February 13, 1945 (24 years old)
The Allies bombed his hometown of Dresden twice in one night. His mother Else and his sister Ilse became refugees and eventually resettled in Rehau, Bavaria, where they arrived on March 20, 1945.

KARLHEINZ STOESS POST-WAR PERIOD (1946-1962)

1946

Joined his mother and sister in Rehau after his release from captivity in the second of half of 1946. He had been sent to England from Alabama for obligatory "de-Nazification" and instruction in democracy before being returned to his family in Germany. Wrote his second memoir, *Eingesperrt! (Locked Up!)*, from December 1947 to April 1948 on the back of American Army requisition forms.

1946-1947

Chief clerk, translator and court interpreter for the U.S. Military Government in Rehau, Bavaria.

1947-1950

Studied German law at the University of Erlangen, Bavaria, Germany and passed the German First State Examination in Law, 1950. The University of Erlangen is where he met his future wife, Irene Misslbeck.

1947-1950

Was a newspaper reporter for the *Frankenpost* and the *Nürnberger und Erlanger Nachrichten* while studying law. Was a member of the Bavarian Newspapermen's Professional Organization.

July 2, 1951

Emigrated to the United States, arriving in New York aboard the S.S. "Washington", one day after his 31st birthday.

Onboard the S.S. "Washington",
Hamburg – New York, 1951

1951-1952
Invoice clerk with the Studebaker Corporation, Washington, DC.

1952-1953
Attended George Washington University Law School, Washington, DC at night. Awarded a Master of Comparative Law, American Practice degree in 1953.

1952-1954
Law Clerk at the law firm of Covington & Burling, Washington, DC. Promoted to Senior Law Clerk during the summer of 1953.

June 11, 1953
Married Irene Maria Misslbeck at St. Bernadette's Catholic Church in Silver Spring, Maryland. They were married in the church rectory instead of the church itself because Karlheinz was not a Catholic.

Karlheinz and Irene Stoess, Washington, DC, 1953

Summer 1953
Worked as a simultaneous interpreter with the U.S. State Department after having passed the German-MSA-Interpreting Test in 1952.

June 1954
Passed the Washington, DC Bar Examination.

February 19, 1957
Became a U.S. citizen. Naturalized at the Circuit Court of Montgomery County in Rockville, Maryland.

April 21, 1957
Birth of daughter Helga Susanne Stoess in Washington, DC.

October 25, 1957
Admitted as an Attorney of the State of Maryland Court of Appeals.

November 7, 1957
Was registered to practice as an attorney before the United States Patent Office.

September 3, 1958
Birth of daughter Marie-Louise Stoess in Washington, DC.

1954-1962
Worked at various law firms in Washington, DC, then at Toulmin & Toulmin. Transferred to their Frankfurt office in Germany, August 1962.

1962-1968
After 7 months in Germany, transferred to Toulmin & Toulmin in Brussels, Belgium (2 years), then took jobs as a patent attorney with Massey Ferguson in Detroit, Michigan and later Burroughs Corporation (3 years).

1968
Transferred from Detroit to Paris, France by Burroughs.

1975

Elected to take early retirement from Burroughs at age 55 rather than transfer back to Detroit. Became a freelance translator of patents and other legal documents (English, German, French) in Paris.

October 31, 1986

Died of Non-Hodgkin lymphoma in a Paris hospital at age 66.

•   •   •

My father once told me that when he was a young man, he celebrated his birthday in a different place 12 years in a row. That now made perfect sense to me.

Fortunately, my mother, Irene Maria Misslbeck Stoess, born August 16, 1921, was still alive at age 96 when I first opened the suitcase, and I could ask her some questions. The Editha Sobbe in question could go to medical school during the war and become a doctor. My mother confirmed that this was the woman I knew as Dr. Editha Finzel (her married name), who had once visited us with her little boy when we lived in Paris, after she had divorced Mr. Finzel. Karlheinz's letters to her were very formal and stilted; he addressed her formally as "Sie" and "Liebes Fräulein Sobbe", only much later transitioning to "Liebe Editha!"

I do not know why she had returned all his letters to her (there was no evidence of her letters to him) but I was intensely grateful to her; I now had a record of all the places he had served up to his capture. As mentioned in the timeline, one particularly poignant piece of mail was an empty envelope postmarked June 6, 1944 (D-Day) stamped "Return to Sender". By the time the letter arrived, my father had surrendered in his bunker on the Normandy coast and his captors had shipped him off to England.

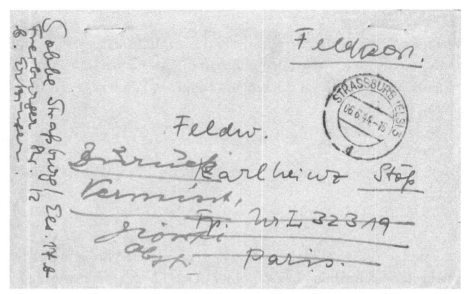

Empty envelope postmarked June 6, 1944 (D-Day) addressed to
Feldwebel Karlheinz Stoess, marked "Missing"

Karlheinz had met my mother Irene when they were both
students at the University of Erlangen after the war. He came from
what was later the country of East Germany, from the city of
Dresden, a city so beautiful it was known as "Florence on the Elbe
River." The city is well worth visiting, being beautifully rebuilt
and reconstructed to look like it once did—unbelievably so—after
being reduced to rubble by Allied bombs at nearly the very end of
the war.

Bombs had destroyed the apartment building in which
Karlheinz's mother and sister lived; mother and daughter had
gotten separated during the bombing and it took them three days
to find each other again. As with the rest of the surviving civilian
population, the authorities resettled them elsewhere in Germany—
in their case, in the small Bavarian town of Rehau. This is where
my father was repatriated after the war, once the Americans
released him and sent him to Great Britain for "de-Nazification",
something every German soldier and many civilians had to
undergo. Returning German soldiers took mandatory re-

education courses in democracy before being allowed to return to Germany.

My father never joined the Nazi party, but his father Rudolph, a civil servant, joined, as did his younger brother Siegfried. It is difficult for me to say why the two of them joined the Nazi party. Rudolph, as a civil servant, may have felt pressure to join in order to keep his job, regardless of whether he shared Nazi beliefs. According to my father, his brother Siegfried was quite an ardent Nazi. Apparently, the brothers often argued about Nazi politics and policies. I suspect that Siegfried most likely was a staunch believer; after all, he held the top enlisted man's rank of *SS-Rottenführer* (Nazi Squad Leader) when he was shot down at 21. Neither of them survived World War II: Rudolph died of tuberculosis (referred to as "pleurisy" by my grandmother in her wartime letters) during the war, in 1944 at age 50, and Siegfried died almost instantly as soon as he arrived at the Russian front in 1943. Of the family only Karlheinz, his mother Else, and younger sister Ilse remained.

From his new home in Rehau, Karlheinz resumed his studies at the University of Erlangen, also in Bavaria, where he met my mother, who was a guest student there. Irene had studied throughout the war, hopping from university to university across Europe to places that still had books, following the professors she especially admired. This was rather normal practice for European students even in peacetime, but she pushed it further, changing universities (and countries) every year. Irene studied in Munich, Germany (1940); Prague, Czechoslovakia (1941); Berlin, Germany (1942) and Innsbruck, Austria (1943). She always thought it strange that most American students spend all four years at a single university. From 1947 to 1948, she was at Erlangen University only once a week, being simultaneously employed as a full-time teacher.

•   •   •

I remember my father as being obsessed with the war, talking about it every chance he got, especially when together with other World War II veterans, whether German or American. However, as I read through the papers, I came to see different sides of him. My father could charm and be a lot of fun: telling stories, making jokes, never one to turn down a good meal, and complimenting his hostesses with the vast amount of food he put away. He could also get furious in a scary way, red-faced and yelling. But he was often silent and morose, opting out of family life and retreating to his room to listen to his scratchy shortwave radio or the classical music he loved.

The contents of the suitcase gave me a whole new vantage point of my father. Little did I know that this battered carryall would become a primary focus of my life for the next several years. Through reading my father's letters and writings, I discovered someone much less withdrawn and much more enthusiastic and participatory than the father I remembered, someone who displayed a sly sense of self-deprecating humor and a distinct romantic streak. He showed the naivete and enthusiasm of youth that one has when the entire world is just waiting to be discovered. Despite the grim reality of war, he had his abiding interests and profound enthusiasms to distract him. He had things he eagerly expected and looked forward to. In short, he was just like any other young person with his whole life spread out before him.

The war had damaged Karlheinz and I suspect he would have received a form of PTSD diagnosis nowadays, and probably one of mild depression as well. To my knowledge, he was never treated with psychiatric medication and I don't think he ever received any therapy. Post-Traumatic Stress Disorder, known as "shell shock", applied only to the most obvious and dramatic cases. The damage done to my father was much more subtle and internal, and he didn't display any outward symptoms you could put your finger on. It manifested itself mainly as an obsession with the war and with the past, at the expense of fully living in the present.

My father, as I remember him, was a dutiful breadwinner. He was very clear that he had chosen patent law as his specialty because it was a relatively unpopular branch of law, one in which he would always find employment. That was his priority, and he suddenly found himself in a field in which the other practitioners mostly had engineering degrees, which he did not. He freely admitted that he found the work tedious, writing patents for obscure pieces of machinery that hardly anyone would ever read. I can't imagine how he could do this successfully in a language not his own, and in a field he had no expertise in. I don't remember him ever expressing excitement about his work; providing for his family was his primary goal.

When I was a child, my father was a source of comfort, the person I ran to when my mother was angry with me, when I couldn't deal with her criticism and demands. He was a place of refuge for a sensitive child somewhat traumatized by constant moves and changes in schooling. I went to six different schools in seven years, starting first grade at age five because there wasn't a kindergarten at the American school I went to when we lived in Frankfurt for seven months. This was obviously not the optimal choice for a physically and emotionally immature, anxious five-year-old.

When my younger sister Marie and I reached early adolescence, we pushed our father away, telling him "Get it yourself" when he asked us to fetch the salt. It can't have been easy for him living in a household of females, two of which wanted little to do with him. This led to a permanent rift and my father increasingly withdrew into himself during our teenage years. I have few memories of him as he became increasingly distant from his two daughters. I don't remember him ever asking about school or my friends, although we had conversations about intellectual topics and things that weren't personal.

I now realize that both sides had hurt feelings, and as much as I wish that he had reached out to us more, I also have profound regrets that I didn't make more of an effort myself. I was not an easy teenager, and of course I didn't have the same insight then as I do now. Sharing many of the same character traits with my father made it even more difficult for me to recognize and change my behavior.

My mother's intellect and their mutual interests of travel drew my father to her; they shared a love of sightseeing, museum-going and long hikes through the forest. They liked to do many of the same things and were quite compatible regarding their day-to-day life, but not so much concerning their basic characters, and they often bickered about inconsequential things. However, they were both very interested in preserving their German culture and language, and bent on not assimilating into the American way of life.

One problem was that my father wanted an intellectual equal, but also a traditional frugal German Hausfrau who would make a comfortable home for her family and who was also an excellent cook and housekeeper. My mother was far ahead of her time, a career woman who had little interest in the housewifely arts, and who earned considerably more than her husband in the last few years of her salaried position at UNESCO in Paris. She undoubtedly loved her two daughters, but was fairly uninterested in what I call "the minutiae of childcare". Unfortunately, she also had a traditional German husband who appreciated the considerable household contribution of her income, but was of little help around the house in day-to-day life. I think my mother's frustrations at home would have been much relieved if she had had more help from my father.

PART II: DECODING

The first book Karlheinz wrote was the one in my sister's possession, *Das Buch Michi* (*The Book of Michi*), which she lent to me so that I could type it in German and translate it into English. It was a love story and corresponded to the one-month period from October to November 1943 that Karlheinz spent in Paris, working at the *Flugwachkommando Paris* (Flight Surveillance Command Paris), known for short as "*Fluko Paris*". He was 23 years old.

To set the stage, it helps to know that the date on which Karlheinz arrived in Paris, October 1, 1943, was most of the way through the German occupation of France. The German military administration in France officially lasted from May 1940 through December 1944, although the Allies had liberated most of the territory by the end of the summer of 1944, following the D-Day liberation of France. In July 1940, the Nazi German forces invaded and defeated France and divided the formerly autonomous French state into two regions. German troops occupied one region, which included Paris. The other remained unoccupied, but had the Vichy regime of General Pétain as its government, which cooperated and collaborated with the Germans.

Karlheinz referred to *The Book of Michi* as a novel, but my mother confirmed that Michi was a real person and that this was a memoir of his remembrances of the single month they spent together. Michi was a *Nachrichtenhelferin*, a female communications assistant in the German *Wehrmacht*. Her assignment was also the *Fluko Paris* during that time period, but she was there both before and after Karlheinz. He stayed in touch with her for many years, and my mother met her as well. We have pictures of her from her time in Paris and from later, when she was married and had a daughter.

The book was nicely bound, with a green-painted paperboard binding. Karlheinz had written it by hand, and it was obviously a final version. The writing was incredibly neat and there were no crossings-out or inserted words. I was grateful that my father's handwriting was so attractive and easy to read. On the title page was a red stamp with the words "CENSORED—Prisoner of War Camp, Aliceville, Alabama". I have since learned that the YMCA supplied the prisoner of war camps with specially printed books and with bookbinding materials to repair the damage from frequent use, as well as to bind the prisoners' own writings.

There was a hand-written "Copyright" date of 1945; Karlheinz had written the memoir between 1944 and 1945, when he was 24 to 25 years old and a German prisoner of war at Camp Aliceville, in Aliceville, Alabama. He probably had plenty of time on his hands to write as he sat behind barbed wire, since NCOs were not required to work as per the Geneva Convention. As I flipped through the book, I could see from the chapter titles every chapter took place in a distinct part of Paris. It would be as much of a travelogue as a love story.

The book's dedication says: *"Für Luise"*, "For Louise". I didn't know who that could be and my mother didn't know either. Just recently, however, I found a reference in my father's war correspondence to a "Luise Michel." I now believe Karlheinz dedicated the book to Michi using her given first name.

All of what follows is a translation from the original German that I did myself, being a former German teacher and raised in a German-speaking home. It was pleasurable work for me. At the end of this first book, *The Book of Michi*, you will find notes on the text comprising additional information, updates and my personal connections to some things my father talks about in each chapter.

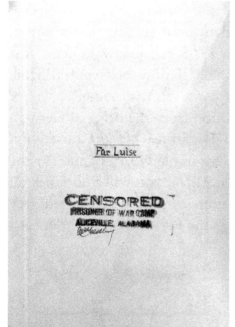

The Book of Michi, Camp Aliceville, 1945

THE BOOK OF MICHI

Karlheinz Stöss

(Translated by Helga Warren)

Aliceville, Alabama, USA
1945

For Luise

[Censored—Prisoner of War Camp, Aliceville, Alabama]

Table of Contents

Foreword

Foreword

I.

It is May 17, 1944.

Slowly, we walk along the Seine. Gravel crunches under our feet; otherwise all is quiet. No light is to be seen, only the moon, which hangs in the heavens like a lantern and bathes the city of Paris and the Seine River in its gentle light.

Over there, in the river, on the Ile de la Cité, one can barely make out the somber, elevated façade of the Notre Dame Cathedral and, quietly rushing, the flowing waters that split at the tip of the island in the Seine.

The mild spring air embraces us both. I take a deep breath and look at her. Her dark hair shimmers, her gaze rests on the ground, and for several minutes now she hasn't said a word. A whispering pair of lovers ducks past us like a shadow and stillness surrounds us once more.

Close to the Hôtel de Ville, a bench invites us to take a rest in the spring evening, and we sit down close together. She tilts her face up to me and her hand rests in mine, like so often before. Why can I only see her for a few hours today? Why can we only be together for such a short time on my voyage from Germany to the French Channel coast? I have just one desire right now, and that is to stay by her side. The eternal, tragic struggle between desire and reality! How sparing Fate is, with the few hours of happiness it accords us...

She speaks to me in her quiet, delicate voice: "It's such torture, that once again you can't stay here. You barely get here, then you have to go away again after only a few hours. And I need you so! Oh, if only you could stay! I feel so abandoned without you, because you're so..."

With this, she presses my hand.

"Yes, Michi, to stay, how wonderful that would be! Like before: four weeks with you in this remarkable city of Paris, which became so dear to us."

Behind us, a late Métro train rumbles out of the ground and disappears, sounding ever fainter on the elevated embankment heading north to the Porte de Clignancourt.

Paris, a spring evening, mild air, the mysterious Seine with its two islands, the pale golden moon, and the girl Michi next to me. Isn't that good fortune? Yes—if you only consider the aforementioned; no—if you consider all the rest: the farewell which will come in only an hour, the uniforms that we both wear, and the war itself, whose most devilish prank yet hangs unmistakably in the air, threatening and horrible: the probable invasion of our Allied enemies into the Continent.

But right now, Michi is still with me. I hold her hand, breathe deeply of her scent, as always Chanel's "Scandale", and look deep into the eyes that are fixed firmly on mine, full of trust and affection.

Suddenly, I see what should be. Seized by excitement, I impulsively throw my arm around Michi's shoulders and cry out: "Right now Paris should stream with light! This city should rightly become 'La Ville Lumière' (City of Light) once again! Thousands and thousands of lamps should light up; the Seine should fill with ships and boats bathed in light, loud with music and song; the Eiffel Tower should shine forth with the light of millions of bulbs, a beacon of the most joyful city of light in the world; and a melody should ring out, the swinging, sparkling melody of light, of happiness, of sheer love of life…"

Michi's eyes burn like mine into the night; our eyes gaze dejectedly across the Seine, between the darkened blocks of houses, the avenues shrouded in darkness, the city squares quiet.

"No, there's no longer any world-class city bathed in light, pulsing with life, like you're dreaming of," Michi says quietly.

"But I know a place like that," I respond knowingly, "a fantastic city, one that even now must still be full of shining light, throbbing with life—New York, the Capital of the New World!"

II.

It is almost midnight, and soon the 30th of June 1944 will become the 1st of July, my 24th birthday.

The ship's engines have slowed for an hour already. Crammed tightly into several stacks of staggered bunk beds, we are lying deep down in the E-Deck of the U.S. troop transport ship "Argentina". Fourteen days have gone by since we left the British harbor of Liverpool, and day after day, we think of that which awaits us in the United States, and even more of that we have left behind.

Indeed, the long-anticipated invasion was a true inferno, just as every clear-thinking individual had expected. After landing on the Normandy Coast on June 6, 1944, the invading troops had pushed far past our military base and at first had left it alone, until they ran out of patience eight days afterwards. A barrage of gunfire lasting several hours, over 50 Sherman tanks, and two battalions of British Commandos overwhelmed us on June 14th. That's how the war ended for us.

How bitter was the march towards the coast without weapons, through the cheering French crowds and the brand new materiel camps of the enemy! How humiliating to have been captured, and to be firmly in the grip of the Allies! It had all happened so quickly: the transfer to England, brief stays in several transition camps, the ride to Liverpool, and the beginning of a vast series of convoys to North America.

All around me, my many fellow prisoners are talking to each other, lying on their bunks. An American military police officer is leaning against the doorframe, propped up on his wooden stick. There—all is quiet! The humming of the ship's engines has suddenly stopped after ten days of continuous operation. We're docked. Undoubtedly in a harbor. But where?

From my sailcloth hammock up on high, I climb down to the floor past two of my lower-lying compatriots. I can't control my urge to get out onto the deck. But I'm not allowed to. There are soldiers posted everywhere. I try to get up there, anyway. I make it past the first soldier on guard and reach D-Deck. Oh boy, Lady Luck seems to be on my side today, because there's no soldier posted on the staircase leading up. Quickly and quietly, I climb ever higher. The fresh air is already streaming towards me—there's a hatch; surely that leads to the deck. From outside, I hear voices. I climb carefully through it—five, six steps and I'm at the railing, close to the American soldiers who have gathered there, who wildly gesticulating and excitedly talking, have turned towards the fascinating sight spread out before us: a city, all lit up! As far as the eye can see, all shimmers, glimmers and glows in the summer night. Light bathes the street; car after car races by, headlights on high beam. Lighted billboards sparkle, skyscrapers glow with thousands of bright windows, and there are ferries hung with colorful, gleaming lanterns. This all unfolds before us. This is what we're staring at: the Americans with expectation, I only with longing. I'm being granted an unexpected birthday gift with this display.

So as not to be discovered and in order to stay here a little longer, I hide behind a lifeboat, still staring out at the panorama of lights. Over there is an American soldier at the railing, who starts singing. I catch only a few words: "Home again... longing for you... Central Park... my New York, my New York."

So we're in New York! I'm suddenly struck by a memory. How was that anyway, with Michi by the River Seine in Paris just a few weeks ago? As I gazed into the darkened city, a vision of a light-flooded metropolis suddenly overcame me. And here I am, the shining city, New York, spread out before me; of course not like a man just poised to hurl himself into the lively New World with abandon, but as a prisoner of war with a worrisome and questionable future, who will hardly know all this light from behind barbed wire, alone and without Michi.

"Oh, my dear girl, how was that with us, anyway?"

Memories of the past wash over me. Thrust face-to-face with New York, this brightly illuminated city, they come to life inside of me...

Flooded with bittersweet, illusory images, I rest my head on the hard planks of the lifeboat. Stay with me a little longer, remembrances of this precious time! I would so like to have my thoughts guided and governed by you! For a long time, I will have nothing but you. Soon, I will have only my memories to live on, come what may, until... yes, until... freedom and life itself draw me close once again.

1.

Paris!

It is October 1st, 1943.

I'm on the D-Train from Cherbourg to Paris, chugging along. What a great feeling, to be transferred to a military duty station in the middle of Paris!

We're already passing Versailles—soon, oh so soon, we'll be pulling into the Gare St. Lazare and I will finally have the chance to get to know Paris, this unique city of all cities.

Rattling back and forth, the train crosses the last track switches into the station. A glass roof, white steam, noise, people, a last hiss and a sudden, lurching stop—we're in Paris.

As I step off the train, the colorful swirl around me jolts me instantly wide-awake and ready for adventure. A thousand impressions surround me everywhere I look, and tickle my fancy in this jumble of a big city.

After a ride on the Métro—that's what the subway is called— where, squished between my suitcases, I gather further impressions from the heavy, competing perfume clouds emanating from the beautiful women, I proceed to my new duty station in the middle of the Montmartre neighborhood. What had I been told? Four hundred female communications assistants, led by only a few Luftwaffe communications officials, supposedly populate the Flugwachkommando or Fluko (Air Force Flight Surveillance Command) Paris. What an exciting prospect for me—I, who come here so unexpectedly from the depressing wilderness of a coastal defense base, I who am so deprived of female companionship!

2.

Fräulein Jansen's Voice

Wow—what a fancy hotel this is, where the offices of my new duty station are located; just a few meters from the entrance, a luxurious urban hustle and bustle flows along the Boulevard Montmartre.

How incredibly lucky I am! My heart thumps joyfully in my chest as I maneuver across thick carpets towards the elevator to reach the floor where the offices are located.

The transcribers are all girls! Only the boss is beaming in masculine complicity, as he informs me I will probably function as one of the new communications liaison officers at the Paris Fluko. They had requested officers for these posts, but since none were to be had, they had had to content themselves with Feldwebel like me (technical sergeants).

My gut feeling is telling me that with this assignment, the gods of war have deemed fit to grant me an incredibly wonderful respite from my usual martial duties. How soon there would be definitive proof that my first impressions were not at all wrong!

Now the Hauptfeldwebel with my marching orders is on his way to me in an adjacent room, through the open door of which I am privy to the following conversation:

"Fräulein Jansen, please assign a hotel accommodation to the new temporary Feldwebel who is to join us."

After a short pause a voice responds which electrifies me, ringing unusually deep and musical, full-bodied and clear, in my surprised ear: "Hmm, let's see, the gentleman was born in 1920—he's coming from the lonely Channel coast, so he's very young and eager for diversion; let's put him in the exclusive Hotel Ambassadeur, in the heart of Montmartre."

What I wouldn't give right now, to see this female being hidden behind the door, who so freely gives voice to all the things

I'm feeling; she possessed of such a melodious instrument, which any famous actress would think it an honor to have been graced with!

But—oh, grave disappointment—the boss himself brings me my hotel assignment from the room next door and I am forced to leave the personnel office, my ears still ringing with the deep and resonant tones of Fräulein Jansen.

As I wait at the elevator to go back down, the door through which I have just departed opens once more and a young lady walks slowly past me. Measured steps, young, tall, superior, noble, self-possessed, maternal—oh, could that possibly be the Fräulein Jansen? How easily could this be the case! If only I could get a word from her, I would be sure! But she is already disappearing down a hallway, and the door to the elevator opens so that I have to get in before I can reflect much longer.

Fräulein "Mischen", Rigoletto And The Beautiful Touraine

Six days have passed, six days during which I haven't had a quiet moment. I had burned with such fervor to get to know the wonderful city of Paris. Inspired by Rilke's "Malte Laurids Brigge", Munthe's "Book of San Michèle" and the "Pariser Zeitung" (Parisian Newspaper), I had long fixated on the French metropolis. And now, suddenly, I can venture forth tirelessly on excursions of discovery, and to visit the sights which have so long preoccupied my imagination.

The convenient scheduling and the simple nature of my work assignment serve me well: Following every night shift in the Fluko, I have two-and-a-half days all to myself before a short afternoon shift somewhat interrupts my pleasant idleness. A short morning shift at my desk follows, then a night to sleep off the duty hours—followed by the shining prospect of another undisturbed two-and-a-half days at my own free disposal.

The Fluko is offering a KdF trip (Kraft durch Freude, or Strength through Joy; KdF was a state-operated leisure organization in Nazi Germany, part of the DAF, Deutsche Arbeitsfront, a German labor organization) to the castles of the Loire Valley. The prospect of seeing these world-famous works of art with my own eyes captivates me. I simply have to go! Oh, glorious Sunday that awaits me!

■　　■　　■

In Blois, the small group of about 20 women assistants and 10 soldiers leaves the train station in the golden autumn sun. The syngas-powered bus is already waiting, and with a fear-inducing rattle we set off along the Loire River through the landscape of

Touraine, the garden of France, where the sight of deep blue grapes draped along kilometer-long vineyards greets us.

After some time, I decide to inspect my fellow travelers, distributed among different compartments on the train ride from Paris to Blois, more closely. Most of the assistants are quite pretty; they are young, fresh-faced girls. But back there in the corner—all alone, as far as I can tell—sits the woman I saw at the elevator in the Fluko Air Command, whom I so want to compare with the vocal phenomenon that is Fräulein Jansen. Oh, what a thrilling prospect! Today I will find out the truth.

I barely pay attention to all the natural wonders whizzing past me, as my eyes continually go back towards the unusually self-possessed, noble feminine face back there in the corner. She looks positively regal! Her thick, dark hair, to which her cap stays attached only with the help of several hairpins, falls to her shoulders. A white silk scarf fills the neck opening of the uniform jacket, which clings tightly to her waist; down the long aisle of the bus, I catch the tender scent of powder and lipstick on her delicate face.

The bus turns into the vast courtyard of a castle. We stop and get out, and the tour guide explains to us we are now in the Château d'Amboise. Everyone assembles for the guided tour, which is about to start. My eyes search for and find "her", a few steps apart from the rest of the noisy, jovial group. She is tall, not much shorter than me, and wonderful, yes, that's the right word—as wonderful as an artful sculpture, enhanced by the tasteful elegance that can emanate from even a communications assistant's uniform, provided the wearer has a sense of fashion. And she distinguishes herself mightily through this sense of fashion. How harmoniously the dark gold pigskin gloves coordinate with the navy blue fabric of her suit! She is also wearing gray-blue sheer stockings and black velvet shoes, and carrying a small crocodile handbag.

Suddenly she turns towards me; she can probably feel me staring at her and how my thoughts are with her. But at this instant, the group walks towards the castle entrance and I'm able to turn around quickly, with no one noticing me staring.

Back and forth, our guide leads us through the rooms of the grand Loire Valley Chateau of Amboise, and everywhere explains to us what happened there during the various eras of French history. He brings Francis I, Henry II, Charles IX and Catherine de Medici to life with his picturesque descriptions, and as he leads us to a balcony and explains that in 1560, because of a conspiracy, a whole row of Huguenots was strung up along the iron fence, our blood runs like ice water through our veins at the thought.

But I'm able to shake free of this bloodthirsty image as a charming sight appears, opening a gate in the garden of my memories. Down there, on the banks of the Loire, lies a small castle. Pointed towers crown both of the side sections, and in front of the main section is a wide terrace with a tremendous wall surmounted by huge stone vases filled with flowers. Behind the castle is an enchanting park with straight paths, fountains, flowerbeds and quiet benches, which almost imperceptibly give way to the forest behind it. A deep peace hangs over this scene, and it brings a performance to mind: namely, the most touching scene from the "Book of San Michèle" by Axel Munthe. Exactly like this castle down there at the river is probably what the Château Rameaux looked like, where Doctor Munthe sat on a park bench with the Countess Juliette one fine May evening. The nightingales fluttered their wings and the round, full moon shone down on the couple, all alone. Stirred by this tender spring evening, Juliette began singing a love song. It is no wonder that the blood of her companion sang as well. For whom would it not have been the same?

The song rang out sweetly:

Non, non, ce n'est pas le jour,
Ce n'est pas l'alouette,
Dont les chants ont frappé ton oreille inquiet,
C'est le rossignol,
Messager de l'amour
(No, no, it is not the day,
It is not the lark,
Whose songs have reached your anxious ear,
It is the nightingale,
Messenger of love)

Now suddenly, just as the doctor, caught up in the evening's enchantment, is at the point where he is ready to confess his love for the countess, an owl screeches in the tree above them; Juliette, frightened, flees into the castle, leaving Doctor Munthe behind and breaking the sweet spell. The full moon appears to be snickering, the traitor. But as if in consolation, a nightingale warbling in a nearby bush takes up Juliette's song of love. It comforts the abandoned dreamer in his unrequited state. The nightingale, messenger of love...

Oh no, my group has gone on ahead without me and it is high time I follow. I throw a last quick glance at my Château Rameaux down there on the banks of the Loire, and at the distant towers of the city of Tours on the horizon, before I step into the dark hallway at the end of which I just see the last of the women assistants disappearing into a room. As I rejoin the group, the guide is giving the following account, during which he brings to life before our very eyes an event from the receding Middle Ages, which had taken place around 1520 in the unchanged rooms of the mighty castle.

"Here in this jail room, the Duke of Grandlieux imprisoned his friend, the Marquis de Bridoré, because his wife, the Duchess, had confessed that de Bridoré had seduced her and led her to break her marriage vows. Shaken to the core by the betrayal of his doubly disloyal loved ones, the imprisoned Marquis scratched the following agonized sentiment into the bull's eye windowpane with his diamond ring: 'Souvent femme varie, bien fol est qui s'y fie.' (Women are so often changeable; without sense is he who puts his trust in them.) Victor Hugo, the great French poet, supposedly read this heartfelt sentiment during one of his visits to Amboise. He had it appear in the same form in his play 'Le roi s'amuse' (The King Amuses Himself), which was performed at the beginning of the 16th century in the court of Francis I. This comedy then became the basis of the libretto of the opera 'Rigoletto', in which we encounter the verse scratched here, at the beginning of the world-famous aria, 'Oh how deceitful are women's hearts'."

Following the guide's explanation, everyone crowds around the clumsily scratched writing on the windowpane. I give voice to my thoughts, murmuring to myself: "Oh, how right the Marquis de Bridoré was when he made such a remarkable, totally accurate comment about what a woman is like. Luckily, we have the oft-performed opera Rigoletto and its fiery aria to remind us constantly of this truth!"

My lady is standing in front of me. She bows her head for a second, turns around to face me, directs a withering look in my direction, and quietly says in a reproachful tone of voice: "How can you possibly agree with such an unfair and narrow-minded condemnation of the entirety of womankind? For example, do you even know how that was in Rigoletto? Gilda sacrificed herself for her lover, the Duke of Mantua. Even though she had to watch through a gap in the wall how he tried to seduce the loose Maguelonne in a bar, after he had sworn eternal love and faithfulness to her, Gilda, she still let herself be stabbed for him. Face-to-face with his proven unfaithfulness and corruption, she still willfully accepted the fatal thrust of her father's weapon meant for him as revenge, simply because she loved the Duke without reservation, as only a woman can love. Do you grasp how great a sacrifice this was? Can you even understand it?"

Under the effects of this rebuke, I'm feeling a little uncomfortable. The only good thing is that no one else had paid attention to what she said. As I was still searching for a suitable response, she had already turned her back to me in apparent haughtiness and had rejoined the forwards-moving group without so much as a backwards glance.

My thoughts are whirling around in my head. This getting to know one another has gone so differently than I imagined! What to do now? So awkward! She had simply felt compelled to defend the dignity and honor of womankind from my attack. Oh, she did not do badly at all! What I wouldn't give to take back my impulsive outburst!

Additionally—now that I think about it—she surely is not Fräulein Jansen. Her voice has a totally different timbre. But then who is she? I have to find out!

Following the tour, the field trip continues. Noon is nigh, and our guide has informed us that there is a lunch waiting for us in a local country inn of great renown.

Right after we enter the dining room of the hotel, everyone rushes happily to the tables set up for us. My supposed Fräulein Jansen also takes a seat; there is no one seated to the left or right of her. I quickly hurry to her left side and sit down. How surprised and amused she looks at me! I have to laugh too, and I introduce myself to her. Even before she can respond, I add: "Until a few hours ago, I thought your surname was Jansen, but when you addressed me in such a 'friendly' manner—how she laughs now!—I realized from the sound of your voice that you can't possibly be her."

"No, you're right. Everyone all over the Fluko knows Fräulein Jansen for her distinctive voice."

She thinks for a minute: "But how do you know only her voice and not her?"

"Well, you know, I heard Fräulein Jansen's beautiful voice from a neighboring room without being able to see her, and then as I was waiting for the elevator, you left the offices in which I had just been. So I assumed you were the owner of that uniquely fabulous voice."

"Well, you assumed wrong," she replied teasingly; "my name is Marianne Michen."

How funny, the way she makes a "sch" sound with Michen!

"So, Mischen, like 'Zucker und Zimt mischen' (to mix sugar and cinnamon)!" I interject.

"No, good sir, I said 'Mischen'." And again she pronounces a full, round, soft "sch" (shh) sound.

"I get it," I say, "it's like the verb 'mischen' (to mix), m-i-s-c-h-e-n."

"No," she shouts with excitement, "'Mischen' I said, so M-i-c-h-e-n."

"According to that spelling, I would say 'Michen' ('ich')," I say, as I let fly with a hard "ch" sound forced through my teeth.

She now thoughtfully rests her chin on her hand, blinks at me rather confused, and says: "See how much I am influenced by my Frankfurt accent! We pronounce every 'ch' as 'sch'!"

"Don't worry, I can't totally get rid of my Sachsen accent either!"

"You don't say," she exclaimed in surprise, "I don't hear it at all."

This affirmation made me smile, as this is a tremendous compliment for anyone from Sachsen (Saxony).

The ice between Fräulein "Mischen" and me is now broken. In the course of our subsequent conversation, every time I pronounce her name with a resounding "sch", she gives a small sigh but then bites eagerly again into her crispy French fries, and with half-closed eyes rapturously drinks the wonderful dark red Touraine wine served from big bottles on all the tables. Because I at least match her in this respect, I soon feel the fruit of the vine coursing through my blood. I am suddenly flooded with happiness. What a prospect: the long ride back to Paris at the side of this girl! As my gaze rests upon her, I notice that she suddenly looks totally different; her serious features have ceded way to a rather restrained and subtle contentment.

We return toward Blois and the bus rattles towards the fiery ball of the setting sun. I actually don't notice anyone around me anymore, because I am totally with Fräulein Michen in spirit. To myself, I am already calling her "Michi", as I have heard her colleagues do. Actually, not "Michi", but "Mischi".

In the course of our conversation, which we conduct quietly with our heads close together, we get to know each other a little better. I would love to know her age. But because it's not socially appropriate to just come out and ask a woman her age, I have to use a little subterfuge, and I say: "Because your overall comportment has nothing at all to do with that of my fifteen-year-old little sister Evelyn, I'm forced to conclude that you are at least ten years older than she is."

"Hey, wait a minute, are you saying that because of my twenty-three candles, I'm no longer a young girl?" She looks at me almost threateningly.

I answer with some hesitation, seeing that storm clouds may soon roll in: "Yeah, well, at twenty-three years old, you're definitely among the older girls!"

Her eyes are shooting sparks now: "Well, well, sticking me in the older girls category, are you! Don't have a lot of tact, do you? And all the while, I still feel so young!"

Long thereafter, sometimes with no provocation at all, she repeats with a pout: "Me—an older girl! Unbelievable!"

.   .   .

In Blois, we're able to find a train compartment with no other members of our party in it. That's the way we like it. We chat in such harmony that nothing is more natural than to arrive at the following conclusion: tomorrow we'll meet at the huge Rex movie palace near the Boulevard Montmartre at 3:00 pm. The "older girl" is history, thank God!

4.

In The Musée Grévin

Who doesn't know the delicious feeling of going to a rendezvous? You arrive 15 minutes early, then anxiously pass the time that brings you ever closer to the hotly expected moment when you finally see "her" rounding the corner, and you eagerly hurry towards her.

That's the way it is now, too. I have prepared myself both physically and spiritually, and wait impatiently and with gleeful anticipation for Michi's arrival. Last night I slept gingerly on the mattress of my large hotel bed, under which I had pressed my trousers with dampened creases, which now hang perfectly smooth and sharply creased from my long legs. In a sudden burst of energy, I've even darned the hole that I've had in the little finger of my left glove for over a month now. And I only shaved half an hour before our meeting. I glide my fingers over my chin as a test—good, very good: "two millimeters beneath the skin."

The big hand of the clock on the Rex Cinema jumps to 3:04. Well, my lady, it would be quite appropriate to arrive now! And there she is. She trips gaily across the lively boulevard, directly towards me. Oh, I haven't seen her look like this yet! She's wearing a light brown tailored suit with thin, dark brown stripes. Strangely, I feel jittery as she suddenly stands before me, but I'm insanely happy at the same time. What a wild, wonderful feeling this is, that courses through my body like electricity!

We greet each other warmly. "Well, Fräulein Michen, nice that you're here! I was really looking forward to seeing you! Could I make a suggestion regarding where we should go?"

"But of course; in fact, I'm really curious to see how you're planning to surprise me."

"Well then, are you familiar with the Musée Grévin?"

She shakes her head no, as the human river of the Boulevard Montmartre swallows us up.

"Well, it's a wax museum where you see everyone from Napoleon to Max Schmeling, from Al Capone to Josephine Baker, and all kinds of famous, well-known, and infamous people from all over the world as lifelike wax statues. What do you say we go there?"

"Sure," Fräulein Michen replies, "that's bound to be a lot of fun!"

As we enter the Musée Grévin, we walk through a long hallway past one large mirror after another, into the center rooms. I can't help furtively glancing into these mirrors over and over, and I notice Michi doing it, too. What is she thinking? Does she notice, like I do, that we make quite a "striking" couple? Of course, it's impossible to tell what a woman really thinks...

Slowly we pass the strange, rigid figures. Here is Pope Pius XII sitting on a richly gilded chair somewhere in the Vatican, receiving several Cardinals who are deferentially approaching His Holiness. At the portal stands a stiffly silent soldier from the Swiss Guard.

Over there, in a big glass case, jovial boozers crowd around the outwardly unimpressively small, but inwardly that much more powerful Napoleon, at a grand ball in Malmaison.

And here hangs the gondola of the stratospheric exploration balloon, out of the hatch of which the thin Professor Piccard sticks his learned head, as a member of his launch team is about to screw the cover shut.

"Look at this gruesome sight over here, Fräulein Michen. Here's Marat, a leader of the French Revolution radicals, being stabbed by a daring young lady in his bathtub."

I notice Michi is uneasy at the sight of this bloodthirstily realistic grouping, so I say: "Okay, let's go on to another room."

That's fine with her. We climb up to the second floor and sit down on two upholstered chairs on the landing. From here, we catch sight of something peculiar. At the end of a dark hallway off to the side, we perceive a dimly lit panorama. The background comprises low-hanging clouds, through which only a few rays of sunlight fall into the room. Three crosses rise from the mountain in the center; the cross in the center stands under a reddish, flickering ray of light, through which the bony form of the nailed-on Savior magically glows. A group of mourners are kneeling beneath the cross.

Michi stares at it, spellbound. "Oh, look!" she says, nudging me and getting up to hurry down the dark corridor towards the panorama. I run after her and stand next to her in front of the glass where she has ceased to take any notice of me, her wide-eyed gaze fixed on the dying Christ. Yes, it's true; this grouping is totally lifelike. The gloomy atmosphere is almost overwhelming. What a singular contrast between the delicate scent of Chanel emanating from Michi's thick hair and this devastating scene of suffering.

Still gazing at Christ on the cross, Michi suddenly speaks with quiet seriousness: "Look here, he died for all of us. His ultimate sacrifice grants us eternal salvation. What would become of us without Christ? Suffering and sin would suffocate us all. But this way we're able to be happy…"

She looks at me earnestly.

"Oh, my dear Michi," I reflect to myself, "this open profession of yours brings us so much closer. What still stands between us, anyway?" With a profound feeling of happiness in my heart, I lightly squeeze her hand. We look deeply into each other's eyes for a moment and then return slowly down the dark corridor, in which the wan light of Golgotha lingers like an omen.

5.

Danger In Dark Montmartre

It is evening, around 8:00 pm, as I walk back and forth in the darkly shadowed entranceway of the Hotel Mondial where Michi lives. Surely she will come soon, although she had gently prepared me that her professional obligations might delay her until around 8:30.

Thick car and foot traffic flows by me down the street and on the sidewalk: good that the bright moon is sending down its rays, otherwise it would be hard to see much of anything in the dark.

I'm in the middle of Montmartre, probably the most famous pleasure capital in the entire world. Even in the wartime year of 1943 there's still a love of life, of rejoicing, tumult and excess. There are so many indications that this is indeed the case: drunks bellow here and there, laughing couples push past, and you can hear dance music coming from all the cafes and cabarets.

And then there's also—oh, a tremor goes through me—here we go! A woman sidles up to me and props herself up against the entranceway. The moonlight fully illuminates her white-powdered face with the cherry red painted lips. Because of the cool, fall evening, a fur coat clings to her tight, youthful body, and a dangling black curl hangs down over her right cheek. She's already quietly speaking to me in French, her eyes gleaming, her teeth shining like pearls, as a thick cloud of the sweet-smelling perfume "Soir de Paris" envelops the whole doorway.

"Hey, darling, come with me to my place; I'm lonely, so lonely…"

Now she tilts her head to the side with beseeching tenderness and digs her long, carmine red nails into my arm. Oh, these ladies sure know what they're doing; you can't deny that to the girls of Montmartre. And they want to be treated with respect, as full-fledged members of the cultivated human race; that's very important to them. Therefore, I answer in the same gentle tone of voice in which she had proposed her adventurous business: "I'd love to come with you, my little one, but I'm waiting for someone."

"Oh, my Lord, that's too bad! Goodbye, my sweet boy!" she whispers, and squeezing my hand quickly and tenderly, she hurries away on her clattering wooden platform shoes.

I'm rid of her. Now, if only Michi would come! Unsettled, I pace back and forth in the doorway. When I'm back on the sidewalk, another woman approaches me, hips swaying.

Damn, what's this? She snuggles softly up to me, boldly tossing her gold-blond hair, and whispers to me with ardor: "I beg of you, my dear friend, come with me, my apartment is close to here, come on, come on!"

She pulls at my sleeve impatiently. For a moment, she lowers her eyes with their long false lashes to show off the bright green eyeshadow on her lids. Her perfume is exceptionally aphrodisiacal. But I have to get rid of her quickly also! Michi is bound to come at any moment, and what would she think of seeing me face-to-face with such a "lady"? Therefore, with all the politeness I can muster, I bend down close toward her and say: "That's very kind of you, my little one, but you have to understand, my dear, I don't have any money at all in my pockets…"

Whoosh, she's gone. Nothing is more effective in getting rid of these creatures than the laconic admission of pennilessness.

If only Michi would show up! Otherwise it will continue on like this, if she doesn't rescue me soon!

Thank God, I hear steps in the doorway; I turn around—it is she, beautiful and fresh, with a lightly powdered face and a faint cloud of Chanel's "Scandale" floating behind her. What a difference between Michi and these floozies! They share a gender—but they come from two totally different worlds.

With a deep sigh of relief, I say: "Do you realize, Fräulein Michen, that you have delivered me?"

"Delivered you from what? You've been waiting patiently all by yourself, after all."

"Sure, at the moment you arrived, but before that I was in deep trouble."

"Why was that?" she asks somewhat uncertainly.

I answer hesitantly: "Because of those determined female Montmartre night hunters."

She suddenly turns red, and in an impulsive, tender gesture links her arm with mine, responding quickly: "Oh, how sorry I am! If I had known, I would have come promptly at 8:00 and let everything lie as it was." She looks down, irritated.

Is it possible? She blames herself for the trespasses of her fellow sex! How gladly would I like to say something very loving to her right now. But it's not time for that yet—unfortunately not yet.

Slowly we stroll in the moonlight to the Metro station to go to Pigalle, to a small cabaret.

Following a short period of silence, she speaks again. "You know, here in Paris, and especially in our Montmartre neighborhood, you experience so much degeneracy, but also so much overflowing love of life. You can only imagine how much I get to see and hear from various of my 400 feminine colleagues regarding this!"

It's obviously difficult for her to continue. But she takes her thought further: "Amid this whirl of supposed happiness, and not wanting to miss anything that surrounds me, to keep to a path that's true to my own ideals—all alone—is sometimes difficult and makes for an inner struggle. Can you understand that? I think I just bared my soul to you."

What an unburdening! Without thinking, I spontaneously reply: "But with your attitude and resolve, you stand out from other people; that's where your individual self-esteem comes from!"

"Yes, yes," she responds pensively, "you're right, but sometimes you need someone to remind you of it. And," she says, looking up at me gratefully, "today you're telling me and I like the sound of that. I'm very pleased…"

Now we're descending the steps to the Métro. My dear Michi, if only you knew how I already belong to you inside! It would horrify you—or would you be happy…?

There are lots of people waiting for the train on the Métro platform, elegant rich people and threadbare poor ones, idlers looking for diversion, and workers on their way to the night shift.

Over there—what plaintive sound is that, back there against the wall? All the thickly massed people turn their heads towards the moaning that now turns into muffled cries. What's going on? An extremely old, quaking man climbs up on a bench at the edge of the platform, still crying out querulously, and spreads his bone thin, trembling hands over us like he's blessing us. His deep-set eyes look disturbed and his scruffy gray-white beard shakes. Suddenly, he loudly addresses the crowd in pastoral tones. Everything goes quiet; Michi grabs my hand, startled; we can hear the quiet whoosh of trains from neighboring platforms.

It's a weird tableau, as the old man now cries out: "I have always prayed for peace, always, with all my heart, and I've seen a vision: peace will come! Soon, soon, peace will come…"

His trembling voice breaks off. A hefty twitch contorts his ascetic, grizzled face and he slowly starts tilting forward. A few women let out shrill screams. But the arms of powerful men catch the falling man. A relieved murmuring breaks out among the startled crowd as they contemplate the crazy man's vision of a soon-to-come peace.

This is what the ugly mug of war looks like! Suffering, hunger, despair, insanity, death—those are its fruits.

Where is your laughter, you idle nightclub-goers; why do you almost miss your train, you night shift workers? Why are you looking at me so sad and lost, Michi? So far, we have experienced little of the war. But the difficult times are still to come, for me and probably for you too...

6.

On The Telephone

I dispatch my morning duties at the Fluko Paris. What a strange occupation! Actually, there is nothing for me to do. It turns out that this job as liaison officer is a real "do-nothing" post. Soon my higher-ups will realize it and immediately return me to the loneliness of the coast. Until that time: Keep mouth shut about the true nature of the non-existent work, pretend to be busy, and use well every free moment that my immense good fortune has granted me in this incredibly beautiful city.

Before being posted here, I could buy two pre-sale tickets to a performance of Beethoven's Ninth Symphony for this evening. How nice it will be to attend with Michi and hear it together! I'm going to call her right away and tell her.

I carefully close the soundproof door of the telephone booth in the underground Fluko behind me, take the phone off the hook, and ask the operator to connect me with the women assistants' office where Michi works.

A voice answers—oh, what a voice!

"Fluko Workroom, Jansen," it resonates deeply, tunefully, and exceedingly elegantly in my ear.

I answer: "Yes—I—I would like to speak to Fräulein Michen; please be so kind as to ask her to come to the phone, Fräulein Jansen."

"But who are you, my good sir? I can't tear my dear Michi away from her work for just anybody!"

"Oh no, Fräulein Jansen, that's not what this is. Why don't you ask Michi if I'm just anybody to her, and you will get a decided 'no'."

"Oh no, my dear sir, you are assuming all kinds of things; I guess you don't know that Michi is very sparing in her affections. Actually, I find you very interesting! Are you the Feldwebel from the Channel coast, twenty-three years old, Hotel Ambassadeur, or not?"

"I am!" I cry, and I have to admit that my heart is beating faster with joy at this unexpected turn in my conversation with the fascinating "Voice" herself.

"So it is you," she continues, laughing gaily. "You interest me because Michi has been talking about you for days now; her tone of voice when she does makes my ears prick up."

I'm flooded with a wave of joy and I say to her with sudden warmth: "Do you know, Fräulein Jansen, that I already sort of know you?"

"No, I didn't know that," she says, surprised.

"I do," I continue eagerly. "I know your voice, which must grab everyone who hears it by the collar; it's of such unusual timbre, it's so…"

"Stop it!" she interrupts me, laughing. "I don't know what everyone has with my voice. Is it really that unusual?"

"It's beautiful, really beautiful!" I cry impulsively, "It wouldn't surprise me at all, if you had something to do with film or stage!"

"That's not quite it, but I'm a reader on record albums for the International Phonetic Association. That's all. But now I'm going to pass you to Michi, who's been looking at me reproachfully for quite some time now."

And here's Michi already, talking to me in her sweet Frankfurt accent:

"Mischen here." Oh, that's so delightful! Again she's taking the "ch" in her name and making a full, softly sibilant "sch" out of it. It's too funny!

We quickly settle on a meeting spot for tonight, and from her voice I can clearly hear how excited she is about the concert that we're going to experience together. We hastily bid each other farewell.

Inside I'm jumping up and down with glee, but outwardly I project an earnest, professional demeanor as I leave the telephone booth and make my way back through the rows of writing, radioing and telephoning female communications assistants to my "work", which—strange as that may sound—is nonexistent.

7.

You Millions, I Embrace You!

Ludwig van Beethoven's Ninth Symphony, Ode to Joy, will forever be an invaluable gift to humanity. One should hear this masterpiece at least once at every stage of life; each time, the experience will be ever richer and more fulfilling, and will lead to an inner purification every time.

The huge orchestra gathers on the stage, the chorus enters, performers tune their instruments, and evermore-elegantly clad spectators fill the hall. The concert is about to begin. Michi is deeply involved in reading the French program about the meaning of the symphony. I gently clasp her slim, white hand, which she doesn't withdraw but leaves in mine with a smiling, sideways glance at me.

The conductor comes on stage and bows; the audience applauds; he turns to the orchestra and taps his music stand; the lights dim; he lifts his arms and lowers them—and now the immortal strains fill the hall, penetrate the listeners' souls, swell in their hearts, sink deep into their minds and tear the veil from a world much more noble than ours, briefly visible to us mortals in those scant untroubled hours of our lives for only moments at a time.

With the last stanza, the choir urges the masterpiece to its thrilling climax. Through Schiller's verses, it extols the power of joy and moves inexorably towards that tremendous exhortation to all humankind:

"Seid umschlungen, Millionen!" ("You millions, I embrace you!"), and onwards:
Diesen Kuß der ganzen Welt!
Brüder—überm Sternenzelt
Muß ein lieber Vater wohnen.

Ihr stürzt nieder, Millionen?
Ahnest du den Schöpfer, Welt?
Such ihn überm Sternenzelt!
Über Sternen muß er wohnen.
(This kiss is for all the world!
Brothers above the starry canopy
There must dwell a loving father.)
(Do you fall in worship, you millions?
World, do you know your creator?
Seek him in the heavens!
Above the stars, he must dwell.)

What an image! That most noble state that humanity can attain is being called upon here.

But what does the truth actually look like? Instead of being embraced, people are tearing each other apart in a world war to end all wars, during a period of supposedly unsurpassed culture and civilization. Is there any example that more clearly reveals how poorly humankind's power of reasoning is faring? Doesn't this abject failure of modern human culture, proven by this inexorably gathering and expanding war, definitively show that our power to govern ourselves, of which we are so proud, means nothing, and that instead there is an even more powerful entity governing the structure of the world, an entity to whom we must all bow down in humble trust and devotion?

This realization floods me once again, and I wish so very much I could persuade others too. Wouldn't that make everything different?

．　　．　　．

Somewhat dazed after the concert, Michi and I wander up the breathtaking Champs-Élysées in the darkness, towards the Arc de Triomphe.

Diffuse moonlight shrouds everything in its matte glow: the widely spaced buildings of the boulevard, the rows of trees, the nighttime pedestrians and the hulking Arch of Triumph, under which the bluish flame of the Tomb of the Unknown Soldier flickers silently.

The mighty Arc de Triomphe is a shrine of the French people. The thrilling words of the Marseillaise, the French national anthem, seem to shine from this memorial of conquest with flaming letters:

Allons, enfants de la patrie,
Le jour de gloire est arrivé...
Aux armes, citoyens,
Formez vos bataillons!
Marchons, marchons!
(Arise, children of the Fatherland,
Our day of glory has arrived...
To arms, citizens.
Form your battalions!
Let's march, let's march!)

As we slowly approach the tomb under the Triumph Arch, we're completely captivated by an arresting sight. In front of the memorial tomb covered with wreaths and flowers, right next to the eternal flame, is an old Frenchman kneeling on the stone pavers. His beret-covered head hangs down towards his chest, he contorts his hands in devotion, and his lips, almost fully covered by a bushy mustache, are mumbling an incomprehensible prayer. He is sadness personified. Taken by the sight, Michi and I stare down upon him.

"Fräulein Michen," (how difficult the formal form of address is becoming for me), "here they all lie, so to speak, all the many, many soldiers sent to their deaths. For what? For their Fatherland, for the glory of their people, for the progress of humanity? Who really knows? Also, your brother and mine offered themselves up on the altar of war. Shouldn't we honor their sacrifice by doing our small part to make sure the world can someday find its way back to peace, to understanding, dignity, generosity and truth…?"

Casting a last sympathetic glance down upon the praying Frenchman as we share in his suffering, we go off into the night.

First, sparks of joy directly from God transported us, and now the wings of Death have brushed us, both symbols of eternal life and the impermanence of the human condition…

.   .   .

As I press Michi's hand in farewell at the entrance of her hotel, I can't leave without asking her a question.

"Say, Fräulein Michen, when I last called you, I spoke for some time with your colleague, Fräulein Jansen, whose voice has somehow affected me."

She shoots me a sharp look. But I continue anyway: "You know, I would so much like to see the person who corresponds to this voice that I know so well. Can you possibly see that I make Fräulein Jansen's acquaintance?"

Michi, who had been listening intently with her eyes fixed on the floor the entire time, now looks me full in the eye. Somewhat hesitantly she replies: "But why not? I'm sure you'll get the chance sometime soon…" Here she stalls helplessly and looks like she would like to escape into the hotel.

But I have one last question: "What does she look like, anyway? I have a definite idea of what I think she looks like, and I want to see if I'm right. I imagine her as full-figured, with black hair and dark eyes…"

"No, no," Michi interrupts me, "she looks totally different: tall, very slender, light blonde hair, blue eyes and…"

As she falters, I continue curiously: "And what else? Pretty?"

"Yes, definitely pretty, but otherwise I can't think of any other distinguishing features; that would be the basics," Michi says, quickly pressing my hand and disappearing through the revolving door of the hotel.

I wander slowly through the quiet streets toward my lodgings. Light blonde, blue-eyed, tall, very slender? Strange—totally different from how I imagined her! And pretty too? But of course, I never doubted that.

Well then, I'll have to see for myself, won't I? Determined, I stride off into the night.

8.

The Fiasco In The Grand Opéra

Afternoon duty in the underground Fluko, the Air Force Flight Surveillance Command. What a welcome opportunity to write a few letters; what a good time to call Michi, who is working in the workroom, to talk to her, totally undisturbed, on the telephone!

Full of joyful anticipation, I close my briefcase, take a dignified and business-like walk to the telephone booth, carefully pull the soundproof door shut behind me, and ask for the female military assistants' workroom in the Fluko hotel.

"Hello, this is Jansen. Who am I speaking with?" rings musically in my ear. A shiver runs through me as I hear my mysterious Voice Queen speak, and I quickly reply:

"This is the man who absolutely has to see you face to face sometime soon. Michi will arrange it."

"Hmm," she answers in a friendly tone of voice, "do you think she will do it soon, and gladly?"

"But of course, I'm sure she will. Listen carefully when I speak to her now, and you'll hear that she's totally ready to do it."

"Well, my dear sir," she responds, "there's just one minor problem; she happens not to be here. She won't come back until 8:00 pm to start her night shift."

"Oh, what a shame," I say, disappointed. "I wanted to ask her if there might be two opera tickets available in your workroom for tonight. I would so like to go to Mozart's 'Magic Flute' with her."

"Oh, too bad for you! And anyway, I snapped up the only opera ticket that our workroom got today, for myself."

Suddenly seized by an intriguing thought, I quickly ask: "So, does that mean you're going to the opera by yourself tonight?"

"It sure does!" she answers in that incredible voice.

"And where will you be sitting, if you don't mind my asking?"

"In the second row, on the right side. But why do you want to know?"

"Oh, that's not important. By the way, Fräulein Jansen, I think we'll get to see each other earlier than you might have thought!"

Unfortunately, I'm unable to hear her answer because someone is knocking impatiently on the door of the phone booth. As I open the door, a communications assistant comes running towards me to say she urgently needs to speak to the Fluko Commander.

So I have no other choice but to call out hastily to Fräulein Jansen: "Sorry, we have to end our conversation, they need the line for a work call!" And I'm already handing the telephone receiver to the impatient assistant.

.　　.　　.

The entrance doors of the darkened Grand Opéra rapidly open and close in quick succession. Horse-drawn taxicabs and bicycle-drawn pedicabs drive up and unload well-dressed patrons.

Somewhat undecided, I step into the opera foyer. Of course, there's the inevitable sign showing that tickets are all sold out, night after night:

"The Magic Flute"—No more tickets available!

Will I still, by hook or by crook, be able to get my hands on such a precious ticket? I know how difficult it is because theater tickets of all kinds are only obtainable days in advance, or through connections. But there is one possibility that can and must work. Momentarily, I will try it out on this attendant in livery who's standing next to the closed ticket window. "Are there any more tickets for sale?" I ask him flat out.

He shakes his head no, flabbergasted at my audacity, and answers with all the dignity he can muster: "I regret to say no, Sir."

"Are you sure about that?" I ask with a smile, toying with two orange-colored R6 cigarette packs that I've just pulled out of my pocket.

He greedily fixes his eyes on them, mumbles, "One moment, please!" and disappears through the door of the ticket office. As soon as he returns, two highly prized boxes of cigarettes wrapped in a hundred-franc bill change hands, for an equally highly prized (at least in the eyes of its beholder) opera ticket. The opera attendant yearning for his cigarettes exits stage right, and the soldier, equally yearning to hear the strains of Mozart, exits stage left. Where to? A glance at the ticket answers that question: second row, left side.

Splendid; what good luck I'm having! My seat is all the way in front, next to the ramp. From here I should easily be able to see Fräulein Jansen, since she's sitting in the second row also, on the right side.

In impatient anticipation, I direct my curious glance around the wide, glorious semicircle dripping in gold. Borrowed opera glasses will help me find her. I scan person after person in the box seats across from my artificially enhanced eyes.

What was the description again? Tall, blonde, slender. I just have to find her. There! That white-blonde shock of hair in the fourth box from the front! That noble, well-groomed face, that exemplary evening gown—oh, that must be her! And her eyes are scanning all around the great opera hall also, where patrons have taken almost every seat now that the performance is about to begin. Who could she possibly be looking for?

I just have to be patient until the first intermission, then I'll talk to her. She's got to be the one, I'm sure of it!

I would tell a lie if I were to say that I paid full attention to the first part of the opera. It's simply impossible to concentrate on the plot and the music because my thoughts are over there with the well-groomed, pretty Fräulein Jansen. What enormous eyes

Michi will make when she hears that I "totally coincidentally" met Fräulein Jansen at the opera! The thought thrills me to no end.

The curtain falls, the lights flare on, and all the doors open: first intermission. With swift steps, I stride across the semi-circular hallway to the other side. The audience is streaming out of the box doors to the foyer to walk around; a few people sit down on the benches separated by marble columns on one side of the long foyer.

My eyes scan the crowd and since I don't see her, I look over at the patrons sitting on the benches in the foyer. Over there, on the last bench, I see white-blonde hair shimmering in the chandelier's light. First, I'll walk by unobtrusively, then I'll take a couple of deep breaths and walk right up to her: that's how I'll do it.

The river of people is slowly pushing me towards her. Surely she knows me from Michi's description, and will probably recognize me right away from my uniform and the decorations of my military rank as I stroll past her.

What a shame! Just as I've almost reached her, another woman sits down on the same bench. Oh, what a horror! Skinny as a rattlesnake, with a knot of stringy blonde hair, freckled face and pale blue eyes fixed moodily on the floor, she just sits down right next to my Queen of All Women, this feminine being so richly gifted by nature, my brand-new acquaintance, Fräulein Jansen, of whom I am already inordinately proud.

Now I've reached her bench. I stay to the side of the river of humanity so that I can slow down and scrutinize her closely.

What a beauty! Michi's attractiveness almost pales in comparison. I understand now why my suggestion that she introduce me to Fräulein Jansen didn't exactly thrill her. She's afraid of the competition! Women are so insightful and cautious, after all.

Now I will finally experience her heavenly voice in combination with her perfect physical appearance. What a glorious moment for me!

I pull myself together, and with the greatest concentration I turn around and stride up to the bench with the two queens: the one of the day and the one of the darkest night (I won't let that one mess up my plans). Without directing so much as a glance at the bony, freckled one, I bow before my golden blonde goddess, who is looking at me with the utmost surprise, and say the following well-rehearsed and carefully thought-out German words:

"See, here I am! Out of thousands of people, I selected you with the unerring certainty of a sleepwalker! What do you say now, my highly esteemed Fräulein Jansen??" Triumphantly, I look down at her and bow once more.

My God! What's happening? She has turned bright red, seems to be at a loss for words, and doesn't know where to look in her boundless embarrassment. And this miserable wretch of a Frenchwoman next to her is grinning like crazy, as if she had understood every word; she gets up suddenly and starts coughing convulsively into her handkerchief. Her shoulders shaking, she allows the rushing river of humanity to sweep her away. What on earth is going on? Bewildered, I look once more at the blonde beauty who is almost squirming with embarrassment, directing wounded looks at me and whispering hesitantly in French: "You must be mistaken, Sir. I am not the type of woman you take me for. I beg of you, please leave me alone!"

I'm almost brought to my knees. It isn't her! I have brazenly addressed a dignified Frenchwoman who thinks I want to force myself upon her. What profound humiliation! Like a wet poodle I creep away, having to witness the promenading patrons staring at me, shaking their heads.

"What rudeness, how forward!" I hear an elderly lady murmur, examining me disapprovingly through her lorgnette. Oh no, no, no—I have to get out of here! How long it takes to run down the enormous staircase! With trembling hands I claim my coat from the coat check and I'm already out on the wide-open opera square, striding off into the dark night with no clear destination.

How refreshing the cold fall wind feels that blows over my hot cheeks. How miserable, this feeling of abject failure! I won't get over this so easily.

9.

A Torturous Hour In The Jardin Du Luxembourg

The day after my fiasco at the opera, I meet Michi at the entrance to the Jardin du Luxembourg. In how many books have I found descriptions of this world-famous garden, and how often have I devotedly read Rilke's story set in the Jardin du Luxembourg and the Jardin des Plantes!

And now I'm going to get to know it myself. Behind the high iron fence lie the wide lawns bisected by paths, trees, ponds, groups of sculpture and flower borders, in which late fall asters bloom with glowing colors.

Here comes Michi! Dressed in a rust-colored fall suit, wearing the most ingenious of Parisian hats (the "dernier cri", or latest fashion), she charmingly emerges from the Métro like Venus rising from the half shell in the foaming ocean, and makes her way towards me.

Look how unusually cheerful she is today! She laughs and beams as if in competition with the autumn sunshine, so much so that it's a sheer joy to look upon her.

After greeting each other warmly, we step through the iron gates into the garden, and leisurely stroll among playing children and other strollers towards the spraying fountains in the middle of the park.

In her almost confounding cheerfulness, the elegant and richly decked-out Michi now starts talking: "It's such a shame that we couldn't go together to see 'The Magic Flute'. My rotten night duty kept me from going, and anyway, Bella Jansen took the only ticket available for that evening for herself, as soon as we got it. So I couldn't even get that ticket for you."

I believe she's looking at me with barely contained bubbling over glee as she continues: "Or were you able to get to the opera, anyway?"

"Yes, yes," I reply quickly, "I was just about to tell you about it. I could get hold of a ticket, after all. I had to bribe an attendant with cigarettes, though."

"Very interesting," Michi muses, and continues in the same lively tone of voice: "And how did you like it? My girlfriend Bella Jansen, who sends you warm greetings by the way, told me she has never enjoyed an opera as much as she did 'The Magic Flute' yesterday evening."

Why have I never noticed how deep the dimples in Michi's cheeks are? She is shaking with barely contained mirth. She can't even walk straight next to me.

"Yes," I respond, "I also really enjoyed the opera. It was outstanding."

"Oh, and I'm supposed to ask you something, too," she continues with an increasingly perplexing lightheartedness, "Bella, who after your phone conversation with her was absolutely sure you would get a ticket, wants to know how you liked the big aria right after the first intermission."

"Which aria?" I ask, confused.

"Oh, come on!" she says with a reproachful look. "Don't you remember? Even I know it by heart:"

In diesen heiligen Hallen kennt man die Rache nicht, und ist ein Mensch gefallen, führt Liebe ihn zur Pflicht.

Dann wandelt er an Freundes Hand vergnügt und froh ins bess're Land.

(Within these sacred portals revenge is unknown, and if a man has fallen, love guides him to his duty.

Then, with a friend's hand, he walks, glad and joyful, into a better land.)

"Fantastic, don't you think? Bella says she was astounded, and wants to know what you thought, too."

As I look at her as she shakes with stifled laughter, a horrible thought suddenly comes to me.

"My dear Fräulein Michen, didn't you say that your friend Jansen has the first name Bella?"

"Yes, Bella, that's right."

"And doesn't Bella mean 'beautiful'?" I ask in a somewhat sharp tone of voice.

"Indeed, Sir!" she says and nods, laughing.

"And—does she do this first name full honor?" I continue, only now fatefully grasping the full extent of the situation.

"Hmm, that's a matter of taste," Michi responds with a mischievous glance. "She has a few small freckles and wears her hair in her own kind of bun and she's extremely thin—but overall, she's..."

"... Awfully ugly, skinny as a rake, horrible!" I interrupt her angrily. "I only knew her voice, so I recklessly jumped to conclusions about her overall appearance based only on that wondrous voice, and therefore... therefore..."

"But I know everything!" Michi calls out in her unfettered amusement. "Bella was sitting next to the Frenchwoman you made moves on and told me everything. We stayed awake all night, laughing so hard our ribs hurt!"

And once again, the comic aspects of the situation have her in their grip, as she howls with laughter and unrestrained glee.

I'm feeling a little sick. What good does the sight of the glorious fountains of the Jardin du Luxembourg, that so many famous men have delighted in, do for me right now? What am I getting out of an autumn stroll in this world-famous park? Nothing. Nothing at all. I'm embarrassed down to my very bones, embarrassed in all the 222 bones of my body.

10.

Herrn Von Rastenberg's Model

Time heals all wounds, especially minor ones; days made more beautiful by a girl like Michi, in the amazing city of Paris, cure all ills with lightning-like speed.

So I no longer have depressing opera reminiscences, as I sit here with Michi in the theater, a theater of the lighter muses, the Théâtre de La Gaîté Lyrique, in which Lehár's "Frasquita" is being conjured forth in front of our very eyes and ears.

It's a rush of dance, light and color, the music alternately stirring us up and calming us down. How distant, now, is the suffering of war that overshadows our daily existence, and how painful the return of our thoughts and consciousness to the gruesome present time.

But we're both still reveling in the melody and have no somber thoughts; how could one, when one is listening to that fantastic song from "Frasquita", that ignites unexpected flights of fancy in every male brain (and surely also in every female sensibility as well): "Darling, I beg of you, come to me tonight...", or as the song in the French text so explicitly states: "Ne t'aurais je qu'une fois..." ("And if I only were to have you once...")

What is Michi thinking right now? I steal a glance at her. Hmm, I see nothing in particular; her face is indifferent, she seems only to be listening to the beautiful voice and not to be preoccupied with the world-famous lyrics of the aria.

Frigidity, good upbringing, lack of arousal, virtue? Why does she remain so unmoved? I don't know. Something is also keeping me from taking her hand at this moment. Actually, I'm pleased to find myself so reticent at precisely this moment. Isn't this a sign that my attraction to Michi has a different source than usual? I know I love Michi. Of course, it's not the type of love that constantly yearns for kisses and tenderness; but isn't it therefore an even greater love, a love that appears to be profound and lasting, one that results from a deep connection between our spirits and our souls, instead of a purely physical urge to be together?

.   .   .

The conversation we have in the theater's vestibule during intermission gives me a clearer insight into my Michi than I have had so far. The experience that she now tells me about explains her being and spotlights her true nature, revealing the purity of her feelings and her noble, innocent soul.

The story came out when I asked her, by chance: "Do you ever go swimming in the big Wehrmacht indoor swimming pool, Fräulein Michen? I went there this morning for the first time and had a good impression of the modern splendor of this, most likely the newest, of Parisian pools."

"Oh, please don't talk to me about that horrible pool, because I really hate it!" she replies, blushing.

"But I beg to differ," I interject. "I have never seen a more beautiful indoor pool than this one. Where else can you still find a marble pool like that, tanning beds, changing rooms like little living rooms, and a café with such an excellent orchestra playing dance music?"

"All true," she answers indignantly, "but if you had had the same experience I had there, you wouldn't want to hear about it anymore, either."

"Now I'm really curious, Fräulein Michen. Won't you tell me about it? You know you can trust me, at least a little."

I have to coax her to speak, as she obviously has some deep inhibition.

She gives me another critical look, smiles sweetly, pulls me into an antechamber of the theater foyer where there are only a few patrons walking back and forth, and begins in a soft voice:

"About three weeks ago, I went swimming in that famous swimming pool with two colleagues. I had splurged on a new, very fashionable bathing suit and wanted to break it in with a few proper dives into the water. Well, the three of us had our fun in the marble swimming pool, and when we were tired of swimming, we went to lie down on the tanning beds on the veranda, where we sort of dozed off. All around us was the commotion of the many visitors, who, as you know, are all soldiers, communications assistants or German nationals who live in Paris."

"Then it happened! Pay attention, so that you know what all can happen to one!"

Strangely, her voice gets hoarse and the look in her eyes actually darkens as she continues her story: "As I lie there on my back, blinking lazily up at the artificial sun, I suddenly feel that someone is staring at me. You know what that's like? You have your eyes closed, but you clearly feel it: someone is staring at you. I open my eyes and sit straight up. Only three meters away, there's a huge, black-haired man standing there, with a thin, slanted moustache and a really hairy chest. As I look at him angrily, he doesn't even pretend to turn away or walk off, but sizes up my body with his eyes for a few more seconds, like a film director looks at the dancing girls auditioning for him, or like a slave dealer looks at the Negro girl he wants to buy."

She gives an inaudible sigh and then asks me querulously: "Can you imagine how unpleasant that was for me? To be like prey out in the open for the lecherous eyes of a black-haired devil, and not be able to do anything about it except blush helplessly? Then this happened: As I was despairingly turning my face left and right to escape his burning gaze, he finally turned around and sauntered away. Relieved, I stood up, wanting to find another corner of the pool facility where I wouldn't run into this lecher again. I had not yet gone, when—imagine my horror!—he turned around again, saw me standing there, smiled insolently and suddenly stretched his arm out in front of him. Already I thought that the shameless one wanted to wave to me! But he closed one eye, holding his thumb out first vertically, then horizontally, sizing me up with his open eye looking over his outstretched arm. I stood rooted to the floor in the face of his brazen nerve. Was this nasty man trying to determine my body measurements? I mean, really, nothing like that had ever happened to me! With great difficulty, I snapped out of my sudden paralysis, ran up the stairs, and sat down at a table at the front of the café near the ramp. From there I could look down into the pool area, where I saw my friends still lying under the light of the tanning lamp. But there! The creepy, dark-haired man was advancing towards them, stopping, and talking to them. Of course, I couldn't hear anything from the upper terrace; I only saw that Gisela stood up suddenly, startled, and stared at the man. Then Margot stood up too, and I watched as the two listened to what he had to say. Suddenly, they started laughing and nodding their heads eagerly. It looked like maybe they agreed with him. I can tell you, I had absolutely no idea what was going on!"

Exhausted, she stopped speaking for a moment. Oh, what a shame. The first chimes had already sounded to tell us that intermission was over.

"Please, Fräulein Michen, tell me the end of the story; I can't wait to hear how it turns out," I say, full of curiosity.

"Okay then, but quickly," is Michi's response, as she rushes to continue: "Once the pushy man had left, I ran down the stairs breathlessly to ask my two friends what had happened. Giggling the whole time, they explained the following to me: this man was the German sculptor Von Rastenberg, who has his studio in Paris. For a big sculpture group he is working on, he has been looking for the ideal model for his Venus. In me he has finally found her, and is begging me to model for his goddess; he won't do me any harm. He is at this pool almost every day and I shouldn't feel embarrassed to just walk up to him and tell him I'm willing, since without my help he won't be able to finish his sculpture."

In the telling, she is reliving the whole sorry tale, and her entire bearing is now one of rage, contempt and shame.

I, on the contrary, am so revved up inside and trying to hide it, that I can only attempt to make my face show the same outrage hers does.

"And what did you do then, Fräulein Michen?" I ask, deadly serious.

"What did I do?? I stormed off! I got dressed and ran home— it was all a blur. And then came that horrible evening in the hotel! All the girls came around and made fun of me! 'His ultimate model', they called me, and opined that Herr Von Rastenberg had excellent taste and really knew how to go about getting what he wanted. Oh, it was simply excruciating!"

We are the last ones in the theater vestibule; all the other patrons are long back in their seats. An usher is already approaching us, saying: "Please take your seats, we are about to begin again!"

We hurry into the theater and get back to our seats just as the curtain opens and the house lights go down.

How happy I am inside! I could jump over all the seats with glee! And that sweet little Michi still has a grumpy look on her face. How sincere she is, how young, how unspoiled! Such an adorable being, such a fine girl! I feel closer to her than ever. Waves of warmth roll over me. Lehár's melodies fill the room, castanets click, gypsies dance on the stage with fervor, campfires glow—I take Michi's hand once more, that long, slim, soft hand with the unreal ivory fingernails, and enclose it with my hand as a sudden wave of tenderness engulfs me. Now the stern edge to her expression dissolves, and she gently presses my hand in return.

As the lights flare back on after the play's act, she draws a card from her handbag, which she hands to me with the following whispered words: "And this is what he gave my friends to give to me. Can you believe the sheer nerve of that man?"

It's just going dark as I finish reading the business card. It says:

Rainer Von Rastenberg
Sculptor
Studio: Paris
23, Boulevard Haussmann

"Bravo, Herr Von Rastenberg, well done, exactly as I would have done it," I reflect to myself. "But," and now my breast swells with new pride: "Please not with Michi! Not with my Michi!"

11.

Zazous And The Seine Terrace In St. Germain

This fourth Sunday in October seems to bring the last mild rays of autumn sunshine with it. The air is of a comfortable temperature and the wind is still, so that the golden brown leaves drift gently into the street, to rest there in colorful disorder as the many pedestrians rustle them with their feet.

How happy am I with this beautiful Sunday morning! Yes, with today's gift of nature, we both absolutely must experience the famous terrace of the Seine in St. Germain. Somehow, Michi and I seem to be blessed with incredible luck; otherwise, our time together could not possibly be so harmonious!

In high spirits, I run down the steps of the Métro entrance, to be taken by subway to the Montparnasse Station, where Michi will meet me so that we can take the suburban train to St. Germain.

How suitable the Métro is for discovering the population components that make up Paris. That's because during wartime all classes of society use the subway: the rich and well-off in first class; the workers, school children and mothers in second class; and the Jews, by decree, in the last car.

As a German soldier of the occupying forces, I can use the first-class car, which, strangely enough, is always especially full. Today it's especially bad. Because I'm only one of many who want to go to the Montparnasse Station today, I have to push myself with all my might in between the French in their Sunday best who cram themselves into the car. Squashed into their midst, I look down on the much shorter French population from my respectable height.

How do these elegant women do it? Even during the worst clothing shortages, they're always clad in the latest fashions of dress and hat.

The cosmetics industry also still seems to run at full production, since how else could every Frenchwoman, every day, have lipstick on her lips, powder on her cheeks, and heavy mascara on her lashes? And this heavy, sweet perfume! You could cut them with a knife, so thick are the aromatic clouds produced by the products of the Houbigant, Lenthéric, Guerlain, Bourgois, Coty, Chanel and Molyneux houses.

That's funny: by chance I find my chest pressed against the back of a young male Zazou. What does "Zazou" mean? Oh, something deliciously decadent! The Zazou movement has its origins in the endless war, the disappointment of the French youth, and the unquenchable drive for amusement even in times of greatest outer and inner need.

There are male and female Zazous. I can see all the distinguishing features on the specimen standing before me: longish hair gelled to a wave in the middle, but combed straight back on the sides so that they meet in back; a brightly patterned silk neck scarf; an overly long, too-big jacket; pants pegged at the bottom; and shoes decorated with fur or suede.

The female Zaszou corresponds to the male in principle, except that her distinguishing features are different. I can also offer you a demonstration of this example, for to the left of me a female Zazou is leaning against the male one, demonstrating the following features: a shock of platinum blonde dyed hair, curled and stacked atop her head; Hollywood-style makeup with a fake beauty spot; garish eye shadow and lips artificially plumped with aggressively red lipstick; a form-fitting suit with a skirt ending just slightly above the knee; and colorful, wooden-soled platform shoes.

Male and female Zazous have two characteristics in common: their very young ages and their ravenous hunger for Swing jazz and Bebop dance music—the more decadent, wild and outrageous, the better.

Michi, being an experienced Parisian, loves the Zazous because she understands this movement and its origins. What do I think? Well...

Hey, what's going on?! Someone is grabbing my left hand!! Who can it be? The man standing directly to my left? No, he's holding on to a leather strap dangling from the ceiling. It's the Zazou girl, pressing her right side against my left one! She has taken my hand in hers, and is now gently stroking my hand, front and back, with her fingertips. Her head is bent towards her Zazou boyfriend, so that her right earring, in the shape of a big white flower, dazzles my eyes.

Whatever should I do? She means this demonstration of tenderness for him, not me! When the dear little one realizes that in the crowd's confusion she has given her attentions to the wrong hand, she'll surely sink to the floor with embarrassment.

Oh, how little understanding I have of Frenchwomen! Now, of course, it has dawned on her what has happened, as she digs her sharp fingernails into my hip and realizes that this hip's clothing is roughed-up military cloth and not the delicate worsted wool of that of her darling. Now, of course, her hand has suddenly decamped. But what does she do? Does her face turn red under its layers of powder? Does she draw her breath in with shame? Oh no, nothing of the sort; instead, she turns around furtively, grins at me shamelessly, and lowers her blue-shadowed eyelids twice in apparent apology. Then she turns to her young man and plants a tender little kiss on his cheek.

Oh, Paris! Oh, you French! Oh, you Zazous! You live in another world from ours. But believe me, you're not as unknowable to me as many with whom I should be entirely familiar... The train slows and stops, the doors spring open: "Montparnasse", the station signs say. Almost everyone gets off. As I exit, I place my accidentally loved hand under my nose. What do you know? It smells of Houbigant's "Grand Filou" perfume. I have to smile: Grand Filou (Big Swindler)! That fits!

"Goodbye, my Grand Filou," I think to myself, "I will never forget you!"

. . .

In Saint-Germain-en-Laye swarms of pedestrians leave the suburban train, lured outdoors by the last rays of the autumn sun, just like Michi and me. Here outside the city, one can enjoy this precious day all the more. How I'm looking forward to the world-famous Seine promenade, which Michi, who has been here before, is now going to show me!

Close to the train station we enter a well-groomed park, from whose tall, old trees leaves flutter without interruption, blanketing the paths and lawns, alternately wilted and crunchy, in shades of red and golden brown.

Michi, who once again is wearing her rust-colored fall suit with the velvet shoes and crocodile handbag that I remember from our first meeting, looks like a movie star. The dark, wavy hair that falls to her shoulders gives her an exotic look, which contrasts unexpectedly and most attractively with her maternal aspect. She has a naturally noble bearing that is reinforced by her sparing makeup and the delicate cloud of Chanel "Scandale" that surrounds her. I am proud to be seen with her and happy that we are becoming closer and closer.

"So pay attention," Michi begins, obviously pleased with her role as my tour guide through the beautiful sights of St. Germain, "back there, behind that iron park gate the Seine promenade begins, which, along with Versailles, Malmaison, Rambouillet, St. Denis, Sèvres and St. Cloud, belongs to the most noteworthy sights of the Paris area. It's a terrace of about two kilometers that runs along this considerably elevated riverbank of the Seine, already put in place during the time of Francis I. All the tourists coming to Paris who don't want to miss a single 3-star attraction in their guidebooks make sure they come here."

We have arrived at the entrance gate to the park and step out onto the terrace. What a view! In front of us is a straight walk following the steep drop of the Seine riverbank. To our left, the woods come up to the walk, which is bordered by rows of plane trees and single benches stretching off into the distance. To our right is a wrought-iron fence along the promenade to guard against the steep drop.

Somewhat hesitantly, we step out onto the terrace to begin our stroll. Oh, beautiful world! What a magnificent view we have from this path!

To the left the sweep of one's gaze runs into the woods, but to the right it swings out into the distance, towards the gently curving silver ribbon of the Seine River down below, the tiny-looking houses on the river's edge, the pastures, meadows and fields drifting off to the horizon in the misty haze.

White clouds have appeared in the sky, which occasionally obscure the mild sunshine, but it continually breaks out again, gilding the tranquil breadth of the river, our avenue with the plane trees, the benches and the colorful carpet of fallen leaves, that together with the fleeting clouds and the mist on the horizon lend the autumn scene a hint of melancholy.

Michi stops walking, places her hand on the railing, and lets her gaze sweep silently over the low-lying river, me, the woods; she now allows her eyes, which mirror the mild sunshine and falling leaves, to wander gently along the path.

Overtaken by the beauty of this moment, I recite to myself the poem that fits so well here, that one could have composed at this exact spot. And Michi listens to me with an interest that increases from word to word and line to line:

Herr: es ist Zeit. Der Sommer war sehr groß.
Leg deinen Schatten auf die Sonnenuhren, und auf den Fluren laß die Winde los.

Befiehl den letzten Früchten voll zu sein; gib ihnen noch zwei südlichere Tage, dränge sie zur Vollendung hin und jage die letzte Süße in den schweren Wein.

Wer jetzt kein Haus hat, baut sich keines mehr.

Wer jetzt allein ist, wird es lange bleiben, wird wachen, lesen, lange Briefe schreiben und wird in den Alleen hin und her unruhig wandern, wenn die Blätter treiben.

(Lord: it is time. The summer was immense.

Let thine shadows upon the sundials fall, and unleash the winds upon the open fields.

Command the last fruits into fullness; give them just two more ripe, southern days, urge them into completion and press the last bit of sweetness into the heavy wine.

He who has no house now will no longer build.

He who is alone now will remain alone, will awake in the night, read, write long letters, and will wander restlessly along the avenues, back and forth, as the leaves begin to blow.)

As I near the end, I see the golden glow in Michi's eyes intensify.

"What joy," she says, her voice trembling with emotion, "I love this Rilke poem [Herbsttag/Autumn Day] so much! After all, I have always been alone! And you know it too; you know it so well! I could tell from the feeling you put into the words. Exactly as you recited it, is how the poet must have felt. You must be a solitary person too, otherwise how would you be able to experience this gentle, yearning song of loneliness in just this way?" She looks at me for a long time, her dark eyes shimmering with deep contentment. Then she places both her hands on my shoulders.

"Du...", I say to her in a low voice using the informal form of address (you) for the first time. "Du," she whispers at first, then joyfully exclaims "Du!" as I pull her tightly towards me.

Falling leaves drift down around us...

．　　．　　．

How long has it been since I was as happy as I am right now? I don't know. Have I ever actually felt as deep a joy as I feel today?

We sit very close together in the dark compartment of the suburban train that brings us back to Paris in the late evening. We see only a few dim lights go rushing by, and the weak little lamp in the train compartment gives off just enough light so that I can faintly see the shimmering contours of my beloved Michi's face.

Today Fortuna has emptied her entire horn of plenty over us, for otherwise, how could it possibly be that we are alone in the compartment and stay alone for the entire journey?

Only now do I learn the entire magic encompassed in the tiny word "du". Only today do I fully grasp what it means to be completely there for one another and to unfold for one another.

It is impossible for two people of the same significance to fall sensuously upon each other and then immediately find their way spiritually to one another. Delicate are the gossamer threads that one must weave soul to soul; gently and carefully does one spin them—but this takes time—it takes time to develop and ripen a love into something noble and precious. This is happening to us now. A lasting, swirling shower of happiness envelops us, that brings our souls together and lets us dissolve into one another, allowing us to forget all that which has weighed so heavily upon us until now.

If only this ride were not ending so soon! We sit together and mostly remain silent. Only seldom does a ray of light flit by as the wheels rattle their monotonous song on the rails; thundering and hissing, a train from the opposite direction rushes by now and then, and sometimes, the whistles of locomotives cry in the night.

Michi speaks and never has her voice sounded so uninhibited and trusting as now. Melodically, word follows word in her familiar Frankfurt accent: "Oh, you know, today I have the courage to ask you for something very special. You will surely agree to it."

"What are you proposing?" I ask her, "If it's something very special, I'm onboard, because I love the unexpected."

She cries out: "Oh, wonderful, then you'll come with me? Listen to what it is: In a gloomy side street of Paris there's a tiny but world famous theatre that's sold out night after night. They perform horror plays there that are unbelievably creepy. I've heard so much about this theatre, 'Grand Guignol', that just the thought of the stories I've been told sends cold shivers down my spine. Without male protection, I don't even dare go there." Excitedly, she grabs my arm. "Will you come with me?"

Made curious by her description, I say: "Of course we'll go there together. But what kinds of horror plays are these? I haven't heard a thing about them!"

"Oh," she says, laughing gaily, "Let me surprise you! I won't tell you anything; you'll see for yourself. When should we go?"

"Tomorrow, Michi, let's go tomorrow; I'll get the tickets and pick you up at the Hotel Mondial."

"Wonderful, it's a deal!" she responds happily.

A resounding, muffled roar replaces the clattering of the rails: We're rolling into the mighty, glass-covered train station, Montparnasse.

We've reached Paris and this fall Sunday without compare has ended; it has become both a symbol and a signifier. What a precious pearl necklace of expressions: St Germain—Rilke—Michi, and the familiar "du"; from now on, only "du"…

12.

"The Rapist" In The Grand Guignol

What strange environs! I am amazed: I have never been to such a small theatre. Roughly 15 rows of seats are in the orchestra area, and a few narrow box seats fill the rest of the theatre. Elegant Parisian patrons take their seats, muffled whispering fills the "Grand Guignol" theatre, and two girls with white lace aprons sell programs.

"Let me see!" Michi exclaims excitedly, as I buy a program.

We both lean over the program to see what awaits us. They will perform several short plays, mostly one act each. The first play, announced with particularly bold lettering, has two acts. It's called "Le Violeur", which means "The Rapist". Oh, what an obscure, darkly promising, disturbing title that is! How can that be something suitable for Michi? I have deep misgivings.

"Hey Michilein!" I say to her.

"Yes?"

"Do you know what 'Le Violeur' means?"

"No, what does it mean?" she asks innocently.

"The Rapist," I answer softly, emphasizing every syllable.

"Oh, no!" she exclaims fearfully, blushing. At this moment, a gong sounds three times from behind the stage and the scary play begins.

It is suspenseful from the very beginning. The stage shows a drab government office with a desk and a file cabinet, where a sobbing woman dressed all in black is telling an attentive judge about the murder of her daughter.

A man sexually assaulted her little girl and then murdered her. Now the trial is supposed to take place, but a considerable difficulty has complicated it: The murderer seems to have gone insane in the past three days. However, the mother of the murdered girl assures the judge that she believes he is faking in order to escape execution; in reality, he knows exactly what he is doing. She requests a confrontation with the murderer.

With increasing suspense, the patrons fidget anxiously in their seats as the court bailiff goes out to get the mentally impaired murderer. The judge and the woman dressed all in black are staring at the door, through which the bailiff suddenly shoves a handcuffed man into the room.

Michi gulps nervously and puts her hand in mine.

A madman is standing on the stage. His wild eyes are wide open and a trickle of saliva runs from his half-open mouth. His head is lolling down as if he had sustained a blow to the back of the head.

The judge immediately asks him why he killed the child. The judge and the mourning mother lean forward anxiously to hear his reply. But he only grins stupidly, gives a few inarticulate sounds, and makes some jerky motions with his hands that rattle the chains of his handcuffs. After a moment of reflection, the judge angrily yanks open a desk drawer and pulls out a blood-soaked girl's dress, jumping up suddenly and thrusting it into the murderer's face. The insane murderer jerks back, wild-eyed, as the mother cries out sharply.

Unease courses through the audience, and Michi presses my hand, trembling.

But nothing happens. The handcuffed man has the blank stare of an idiot and seems to look right through the bloodstained dress.

The mother of the murdered child suddenly cries out: "He's not crazy, he's just pretending! Can't you see that he's playacting? He's not insane! No, not at all! He's not at all insane!"

It's the end of the first act and the curtain quickly comes down.

As the lights come on briefly, the deeply anxious patrons are murmuring among themselves. How will this go on? Is he crazy?

Or isn't he? What will we find out? These are the questions the audience now grapples with.

And what does Michi have to say? Nothing. Right now, she is nervously wiping her forehead with her handkerchief. Oh, my darling girl, have you taken on more than you can handle, with the horror plays of the Grand Guignol?

As darkness descends, she quickly puts her hand in mine again. That seems to agree especially well with her today.

The opening curtain reveals a jail cell with two beds. Weak daylight from a barred window faintly illuminates the cell. A moaning prisoner occupies one of the two cots. There is no one else in the cell. He turns fitfully back and forth; suddenly he stands up. A wrinkled prison suit covers his slight frame. His hair is standing on end; his two empty eye sockets dominate a frightened, unshaven face: He is blind.

With his fingertips held out in front of him, he runs around the cell as if being chased. Then he stumbles towards his cot and rummages around in his straw mattress with trembling hands until he produces a long, pointy metal file; he kisses it with delight, climbs onto a stool, and holds it against the metal bars of the window as if testing it. But suddenly there is a jingle of keys outside the door. He startles on his stool as if he had felt the lash of a whip, almost falls off, and barely gets the file back into the straw mattress before a prison guard shoves a new prisoner into the cell, with the words: "So you're going to stay here, you madman!"

Who is it? The insane murderer! He stumbles in, crazy-eyed, with his now familiar posture of forward-hanging head and open mouth, stopping still in the middle of the cell. Behind him, we hear a key turning in the lock and heavy steps retreating down the hall; the blind prisoner and the insane one are now alone.

Since the moment the murderer crossed the threshold, the blind man has been sitting in a hunched, protective posture on his cot, his blank face twitching convulsively. The madman stares at him fixedly, with no change of expression on his idiotically contorted face.

Suddenly the blind man addresses him in a hollow voice: "Who are you? What have you done?"

The madman says nothing.

The blind man pauses briefly and speaks again, this time more forcefully and insistently: "Tell me who you are. Can't you see I'm blind? I can hear you breathing!"

The idiot reacts as if someone had dealt him a blow: His face tightens; he lifts his head, closes his mouth and wipes the spittle off with the back of his hand. His eyes return to normal, and with a deep breath, he advances slowly on the blind man.

"Who am I? You want to know? Oh, that's not in the least important. I'm here because I have a little murder on my conscience. But what about you? Have you been in this depressing cell for long?"

The blind man twitches as if having a seizure and answers tearfully: "It's already been six long years and I still have eight to go. And I'm blind, blind, I tell you!" He covers his empty eye sockets with his hands in despair. "Do you know what that means? No, of course not! You can't know!" he shouts. "Can you see the sun?"

"Yes, of course!"

"And the flowers, the trees, the houses?"

"Naturally!"

"And the open fields, all the many, many colors?"

"Yes, yes, yes!" the murderer screams, who, since he has discovered that he's dealing with a blind man, shows no trace of insanity anymore.

At this moment, we hear loud steps in the prison hallway, a clutch of keys rattles, the door to the cell springs open, and two men enter. It is the judge from the first act and a gentleman in a white coat, most likely a doctor.

Oh, what a transformation the murderer undergoes, as soon as he hears the key in the lock of the jail cell! In no time, he has transformed back into a madman. He slumps dejectedly on his bed in his former posture of hanging head, half-open mouth and crazed eyes, not paying any attention to the two new arrivals. They look at him with concern and the judge says to the doctor: "See, that's the murderer who has lost his mind since the day of the murder. But we have every reason to believe that he's faking; he's most likely just pretending."

"So then, I'm going to inspect him more closely," says the doctor as he steps closer.

But there is no change in the murderer's expression. He continues to sway back and forth in a crouching position on his cot: he looks, for all the world, like a true madman.

"Hmm," the doctor says thoughtfully, resting his hand on his chin, "we're going to have to conduct an intensive observation."

The two men turn and leave the cell.

The blind man has been intensely following this exchange the entire time. As the steps in the corridor grow fainter and fainter, the murderer abruptly puts an end to his charade and starts pacing back and forth in the cell, whistling softly to himself.

After a few moments, the blind man speaks once again in a hollow voice: "Oh, so that's how it is with you. You want to walk free with your deceitful behavior, you want to see the world once more: the flowers, the trees, the people, the sun..." He raises his voice to a shout with each enumeration of what the other will see again. He gets up and holds his trembling arms up in the air.

The murderer, gritting his teeth, shouts: "Leave me alone with your hysterical screaming. I hope you rot in this cell. But I, I, I will walk free!"

The face of the blind man suddenly contorts itself into a dreadful grimace; he reaches into his straw mattress, pulls out the metal file, and holds it triumphantly up in the air. He now screams as if possessed: "What? I should die in here?" He gives a hoarse laugh. "Me, **I'm** going to be free. You're the one who will despair, because I'm going to tell everyone about the trick you're playing!!" He screams this last sentence shrilly at the murderer.

The latter now crouches down and creeps cat-like towards the blind man. With his acute sense of hearing, however, the former hears the soft steps and stumbles backwards, and using the cell wall as a support, he holds up the file like a dagger, ready to deal the fatal blow. At the same time he hisses: "If you try to attack me, I will stab your eyes out, you, you..." Trembling, he pushes back against the wall.

Following a moment of reflection, the murderer slowly and quietly crawls on all fours towards the blind man...

Audience suspense has reached a low boil. Michi moans softly and anxiously presses my hand. How will this possibly end?

By now the murderer has reached the feet of the blind man with his hands and suddenly grabs his ankles, so that the blind man falls on his back. The two wrestle angrily on the floor. As the murderer tries to wrest the file from the blind man, the latter breathlessly, haltingly screeches: "Never again—will you—see, see the sun, never again..."

He is gaining the upper hand in the wrestling match, an outcome one would never have guessed from the sight of his emaciated frame. What's this? He has suddenly flipped the murderer onto his back, is kneeling on his chest, is pressing his left hand over the eyes of his opponent, and now drives the file with his right hand through his open fingers, right into the eyes of his prey! A huge cry of pain and despair echoes throughout the theater. Blood pools under the hand of the attacking blind man, and the curtain quickly falls.

Michi is about to faint. With tears in her eyes, she stands up and says to me: "Quick, let's get out of here! I can't take it anymore…" We rapidly leave the theatre as the audience slowly emerges from its stupor and applauds wildly.

As I help Michi into her coat at the coat check, the doors are about to close again: the next murder play, "The Sleeping Woman", is about to begin. Michi has had enough of these offerings, however. Oh, does she ever regret her excessive curiosity, which has led her to step into one of the notorious "cesspools" of this world-renowned city!

.　　.　　.

She's still trembling as we walk through the silent, night-darkened street. "Say," she says emotionally, "what we just saw was awful! Without you, I wouldn't ever be able to regain peace again. You know, I always have to be led and guided in life. I need someone who holds me tight, whom I can look up to, whom I trust absolutely. Do you understand what I'm saying?"

"Of course I understand, Michi!" At the same time I link my arm firmly with hers and pull my beloved girl close to me as we wander slowly through the deserted streets: "Do you know how dearly I would like to be the one who leads and guides **you**?"

She is still trembling as she responds: "Does that mean you would marry me, just as I am?"

"Yes," I answer with emphasis, plain and simple.

She takes a deep breath and stays silent for a few seconds, then speaks slowly, emphasizing each word: "When the war is over—and if you still want me—I would say yes."

What is this exhilarating feeling that sweeps over me? Is it possible? Dare I throw my hat into the ring for Michi? Can I dare to, even though I'm a very young man with no profession, rank, honors, title, or money? Can I possibly hope for Michi, a girl one could imagine only with a successful business executive, academic, or staff officer?

How precious this life is, to grab hold of! Oh, beautiful, marvelous world!

She speaks again. Quietly and thoughtfully, almost to herself, she says: "I have always thought that if I were to be swept into the arms of a man by pure passion, I would lose myself, because that feeling couldn't possibly last forever and form the basis of a lasting relationship. But if I truly love with my heart and soul like I do now, then I'm on the right path. I feel it clearly. I'm so excited about the future! We two now have a goal that's worth waiting for."

So you really can experience something like this, have it happen to you! Up to now, I had thought you could only hope for and dream of such things. But this amazing girl of flesh and blood has inspired me. She brings such joy to my life. And that is worth so much, so very much.

Before we take leave of one another, I suddenly have an idea: "Hey Michi, on Sunday is Reformation Day. Shall we go together to the service in the church of the German expatriates? I would love to go to church with you sometime."

"Oh, what a great idea!" she responds enthusiastically, and it looks like the nightmare that was "The Rapist" has definitively receded.

13.

The Reformation Day Celebration

Even on this last day of October, the sun sends down its gentle, golden rays. The wide boulevard stretches out before us, down which expatriate Germans, nuns, female communications assistants and soldiers make their way to the Reformation Day service of the church of the German Lutheran community. Over there, ahead of us, we see its graceful steeple, from which emanates the clamorous ringing of bells calling the faithful.

Michi is beaming again, as is her wont on Sundays. She seems to me to be especially cheerful today. Every once in a while she gives me a sideways glance, smiles to herself, and kicks at the crumpled leaves lying brightly colored in the street with the tips of her shoes.

By now, we have reached the church entrance and we go inside. The nave rises high above us, and gentle sunlight streams through the dome windows of the crossing onto the altar, on which our Savior with his crown of thorns hangs beseechingly upon the cross.

Once again, like that time in the Musée Grévin, I see Michi direct her gaze towards Christ; her eyes have a strange sheen to them and she looks straight ahead without uttering a word.

After the homily, given by a military chaplain, the congregation sings the Reformation Hymn of the Lutheran church. As always, this is a moving experience, as we sing this hymn with a great deal of ardent feeling. The defiant stanzas, accompanied by thundering organ music, ring throughout the church:

Ein' feste Burg ist unser Gott,
Ein' gute Wehr und Waffen.
Er hilft uns frei aus aller Not,

Die uns jetzt hat betroffen...
Mit unsrer Macht ist nichts getan,
Wir sind gar bald verloren;
Es streit' für uns der rechte Mann,
Den Gott hat selbst erkoren.
Fragst du, wer der ist?
Er heißt Jesus Christ...
Und wenn die Welt voll Teufel wär'
Und wollt' uns gar verschlingen,
So fürchten wir uns nicht so sehr,
Es soll uns doch gelingen...
Nehmen sie den Leib,
Gut, Ehr', Kind und Weib:
Laß fahren dahin,
Sie haben's kein' Gewinn,
Das Reich muß uns doch bleiben.

(A mighty fortress is our God,
A bulwark never failing;
Our helper, He amid the flood
Of mortal ills prevailing...)
(Did we, in our own strength, confide,
Our striving would be losing;
Were not the right Man on our side,
The Man of God's own choosing:
Dost ask who that may be?
Christ Jesus, it is He...)
(And though this world, with devils filled, should threaten to undo us,
We will not fear, for God hath willed
His truth to triumph through us...)
(The spirit and the gifts are ours
Through Him who with us sideth:
Let goods and kindred go, this mortal life also.
The body they may kill:

God's truth abideth still,
His Kingdom is forever.)

Since Michi first saw Christ on the cross, she has undergone a change: she seems to have fallen under the spell of another world, and I am careful not to interrupt her reverie with an ill-timed utterance.

At the end of the service, the chaplain addresses the faithful once more and proclaims: "We will now celebrate the sacred meal. We invite all who feel themselves called to the Lord's Table to take part, in the name of Jesus Christ."

Michi takes my arm and, with shining eyes, says to me: "Please, let's stay! I would so like to take Holy Communion with you!"

Only a few members of the congregation come up to the altar, on which the two chaplains have prepared the sacred meal.

Sun streams through the stained glass windows, and the organ plays quietly as the celebration begins.

Being seated towards the back, we are the last to arrive at the altar, just the two of us. Michi stands to my right on the soft carpet. The organ plays louder, and the sun floods down in broad, bright stripes into the inner sanctum. We are both deeply affected by the wonder of this meaningful moment, which I wish with a burning heart would prove to be a symbolic portent.

One chaplain gives the host first to Michi, then to me, and says: "Take it and eat it; this is the Body of Christ, given for you."

And the other pastor, with the silver chalice, which he sets to our lips, continues: "Take it and drink it; this is the Blood of Christ, shed for you and for the forgiveness of sins."

As we go back to our pew, Michi gently places her hand under my arm. Oh, she undoubtedly feels the same symbolic weight of this moment and probably has the same impression of it as I have. But we don't speak of it; we stay silent and we are happy.

14.

Tears Fall In My Heart

On the 2nd of November, as I tranquilly set down my letter pad to begin my morning duty at the Fluko, I am ordered to see the Fluko Commander.

Unsuspecting, I enter his office.

"I just received a telex message," he begins in a professionally neutral tone, "that you are being recalled to your duty station on the Channel coast. Your assignment with us has, therefore, ended. I thank you for your service. Tomorrow you will go back."

Following this laconic speech, he looks at me coldly and unaffectedly, as if he had just said the most natural thing in the world. Of course, he can't possibly know how this news is affecting me; he would never in his wildest dreams realize that I'm experiencing a stab through the heart and my pulse is pounding as if about to burst!

With a hoarse "Jawohl, Herr Hauptmann (Captain)!" I leave his office, pack up my briefcase, sign out with the duty officer and stumble out of the underground hallways of the Fluko into the fresh air.

A short while later, I reach the Place de la Concorde. Oh no, it's suddenly raining. Gusts of wind whirl towards me, carrying fat drops of rain and wet leaves.

What do you think, you old Obelisk of Luxor, quarried in ancient Egypt over three thousand years ago, you who now stand at the spot where the fearful guillotine reigned during the French Revolution?

But the Obelisk of Luxor, which has proudly stood in the middle of the Place de la Concorde for a good hundred years, says nothing. Drops of rain drain off its polished sides adorned with hieroglyphics, as its tip pierces the patchy fog that is enveloping the broad plaza.

Over there, in the rainy mist, are the Tuileries Gardens and right behind them flows the Seine. A few minutes later I have reached its banks and I stare into the dark, occasionally gurgling waters. You, Old River, made so famous by your location in this renowned world city, what various fates have you witnessed? How many people have wandered your banks with their worries and miseries? And how many of them became the "Inconnue de la Seine" (The Unknown Woman of the Seine) besides the one known the world over?

"When will I be together with Michi again?" I ask in despair. But the rushing waters yield no answer.

The rain falls harder and harder, and the raindrops hammer monotonously on the wetly gleaming tin roofs of the green boxes of the bouquinistes that I pass along the banks of the Seine.

But the rain doesn't bother me! It's probably making fun of me right now, as it runs slowly into my collar and drips down my neck. What do I care, anyway! I'm not even going to go around this big puddle, but right through it instead. Splash—splash— splash and my socks are wet.

My thoughts circle around Michi repeatedly. I'm pretty sure I won't see her again so soon. Maybe for a few hours on my way to vacation or on a business trip. But these hopes are so vague and unformed. Won't this war end up cancelling out my pathetic, modest calculations? Without a doubt, it will escalate hugely in the coming year, because of the long-awaited Anglo-Saxon invasion of Western Europe. Then for us men comes the fighting, and maybe for very many, also the dying; for Michi comes the flight back to her homeland. And what will come after that? This is where my ridiculous meditations on the future break down— it's about time. What match am I, with my feeble capabilities, for this unholy war, which destroys not only my most fervent hopes?

At this moment, the wind blows a huge maple leaf into my face. Nonplussed, I take it between my fingers, stand still, and murmur thoughtfully to myself: "What am I saying, that this unholy war will destroy my most fervent hopes? That's not quite fair! Didn't this apparently so brutal a war drive Michi into my arms? Do I even know if maybe once again it means well with me, by taking me away from her? Maybe the gods of war have special plans for Michi and me, separating us only now that we have had sufficient time to get to know one another."

Do they want to give us a probationary period to prove our love to each other? Is this separation perhaps the solid foundation on which we will find our way back to each other in the future?

How strange: Renewed hope flares up in me, and suddenly I feel like what's happening to me is no ending, but just a temporary pause.

As I return, soaking wet, to my hotel room sometime later, melancholy overtakes me again. It probably has to do with my impersonal surroundings and the drip-drip-drip of the rain outside.

I open the door to the closet to take out all my things and pack them into my suitcase. Once I have taken everything out and spread it on the bed, the table and the chairs, I reach into the closet shelves again to make sure there is nothing left. On the topmost shelf I feel something flat against my fingertips, in the very back. I reach for it and take it out. It's a small, dusty book that I look at carefully. "Choix de Poésies Lyriques" (Collection of Lyric Poetry) is the title. It doesn't even belong to me; one of my predecessors must have left it here, maybe a long time ago.

I pull back the curtain at the window and look out now and again while I slowly leaf through the book. The rain thunders down into the street, occasionally whipped into surging clouds of mist by the wind. The raindrops pound the tin floor of the tiny balcony outside my room.

Poems by Hugo, Musset, Chénier, Maupassant, Baudelaire and other French lyric poets are in the collection. And here, here comes Verlaine, Paul Verlaine, who is so familiar to me. Of course, like with all anthologies, the selection here begins with "Romances Sans Paroles" (Songs Without Words).

Greedily, my senses drink in the verses. They encapsulate the entirety of my sorrow about the upcoming separation from Michi, the pain of my departure from Paris, and the continuous sound of the pounding, falling, dripping rain outside...

Il pleure dans mon coeur
Comme il pleut sur la ville;
Quelle est cette langueur
Qui pénètre mon coeur?
Ô bruit doux de la pluie
Par terre et sur les toits!
Pour un coeur qui s'ennuie
Ô le chant de la pluie!
(Tears fall in my heart like rain falls on the town;
What is this languor which pervades my heart?)
(Oh, the soft sound of the rain on the ground and the roofs!
For a listless heart, oh, the song of the rain!)

I look up and stare out at the rain: Il pleure dans mon coeur come il pleut sur la ville... tears fall in my heart like rain falls on the town...

The End

Notes on the Text: The Book of Michi

Foreword

Karlheinz was stationed in Paris for one month, from the beginning of October until the beginning of November 1943, which is where he first met Michi. After that, he was stationed in Luc-sur-Mer on the Normandy coast, his last duty station, before being taken prisoner. He had one last leave granted in April 1944, during which he went home to Dresden to visit his family. It was on May 17, 1944, that he passed through Paris on his way back to the Normandy coast and saw Michi for a few hours. This passage hints at the invasion to come on June 6th.

The British captured Karlheinz eight days after D-Day, transferred him to Liverpool, and transported him to New York as a prisoner of war. He arrived in New York on July 1, 1944, his 24th birthday.

He talks about the soldiers sleeping in bunks or beds on the ship, but then mentions his "sailcloth hammock". Apparently hammocks as sleeping accommodations were common on the prisoner transport ships, maybe also for reasons of weight, but primarily for ease of installation in huge cargo hold areas where it was easier to hang hammocks rather than install bunk bed frames on curved walls.

It is interesting that Karlheinz wrote about falling in love with Michi and his lovely month in Paris, a city he had always wanted to visit, rather than his wartime experiences and subsequent capture, during the time he was being held as a prisoner of war in America. He only wrote about those experiences in his second memoir when he was back in Germany. Maybe the "remembrances of this precious time" are what sustained him in captivity and allowed him a mental escape from his drab, new reality.

Chapter 1: Paris!

Karlheinz was supposed to be posted in Bayeux on the Normandy coast, but received an unexpected (and thrilling) change of orders to Paris. He stays in Paris for exactly one month, the month of October, and his entire relationship with Michi will take place in that one month.

Chapter 2: Fräulein Jansen's Voice

In this and the previous chapter, Karlheinz is talking about the *Nachrichtenhelferinnen*, the female communications assistants of the German *Wehrmacht*. At the beginning of the war, women in Nazi Germany were not involved with the *Wehrmacht*, as Hitler was ideologically opposed to conscription for women. But because so many men were being sent to the Front, the Wehrmacht brought in women in auxiliary positions. By 1945, some 500,000 women were serving as *Wehrmachtshelferinnen* (female Wehrmacht assistants) in the capacity of transmission operators, administrative clerks, anti-aircraft defense employees or volunteer nurses. About half had "volunteered" for military service, while the other half performed obligatory services connected to the war effort, similar to being drafted.

Karlheinz never uses this term in his writings, but these female helpers were nicknamed *Blitzmädchen* (or Blitzmädel in the Bavarian dialect), sometimes meant derogatorily. This means "lightning bolt girls", and they were named after the double lightning bolt symbol on their uniforms (the same lightning bolt symbol as on SS uniforms).

Chapter 3: Fräulein "Mischen", Rigoletto And The Beautiful Touraine

Karlheinz arrived in Paris on October 1st, 1943 and it is now six days later, so October 7th. From here on, every chapter takes place in a distinct part of Paris or its surroundings, and it will become clear that the book is every bit as much a travelogue as a love story.

My father mentions the group traveled in a "syngas-powered bus". Syngas, also known as synthesis gas, is a fuel gas mixture consisting primarily of hydrogen, carbon monoxide, and very often some carbon dioxide. It can be a product of coal, wood or biomass gasification and can be used as a fuel for internal combustion engines. The Europeans, especially the Germans, used it used it widely during World War II to compensate for gasoline shortages. Today, syngas made from biomass (crop waste, for example) is appreciated as an eco-friendly fuel.

The book mentioned by Karlheinz, *The Story of San Michèle*, is a book of memoirs by Swedish physician Axel Munthe, originally written in English and first published in 1929. It was a bestseller in many languages and is continually being republished. Munthe was an ardent animal lover, and several discussions and interactions with animals take place in his book, such as that with the operatic nightingale who takes up Countess Juliette's song of love.

Chapter 4: In The Musée Grévin

Karlheinz and Michi meet at the Grand Rex Cinema, a lovely art déco *monument historique* (historical landmark) that is still in operation today. It is a scale model of the famous Radio City Music Hall in New York City. Opened in December 1932, the German Wehrmacht requisitioned it during the Occupation, and turned it into a *Soldatenkino* (soldiers' cinema) for German soldiers on leave. I see no evidence of the clock under which Karlheinz and Michi met on either historic or modern images.

The Musée Grévin still exists today; one can compare it to Madame Tussaud's Wax Museum. It has a splashy website and concentrates mostly on celebrities these days: entertainers, politicians and sports figures.

Chapter 5: Danger In Dark Montmartre

The Montmartre arrondissement of Paris, and especially the Pigalle district (sometimes called "Pig Alley"), are still so-called raunchy areas in the present day. As of April 2016, soliciting sex (prostitution) is still legal in France, although the surrounding activities, such as brothels (known as "bordelles"), or pimping, are illegal. Since this law of April 2016, clients of prostitutes also face criminal prosecution. France outlawed brothels in 1946 after World War II, partly because of their wartime collaboration with the Germans during the occupation of France. There were 1500 brothels across the country with 177 in Paris alone; the Germans commandeered some of the Paris brothels for their exclusive use. The ladies who solicited Karlheinz were streetwalkers or independent contractors, if you will. Obviously, they targeted lonely young German soldiers far away from home.

Chapter 6: On The Telephone

Karlheinz was not alone in being excited to attend a performance of Beethoven's Ninth Symphony. It is Beethoven's most famous symphony, along with the Fifth, and was longer and more complex than any symphony he had written. It also required a larger orchestra. Another unique feature was that it included a chorus and vocal soloists in the last movement, a first for a symphony. I unfortunately do not share Karlheinz's deep knowledge of and love for classical music and have never heard this symphony in its entirety myself.

Chapter 7: You Millions, I Embrace You!

Further to the symphony: Beethoven's Ninth is about 70 minutes long; Friedrich Schiller's poem "Ode to Joy", set to music and sung by a chorus, comprises the fourth and final movement of the symphony. Beethoven was almost entirely deaf when the piece was first performed in 1824 and could hardly hear the thunderous applause from the audience. Some viewed the symphony as a statement of freedom in the repressive political environment of Europe. The poem *Ode to Joy* represents the triumph of universal brotherhood over war and desperation. This poem that Beethoven put to music praises and wishes for freedom and peace among all peoples. The Frenchmen Karlheinz and Michi encounter in the Métro and at the Arc de Triomphe personify these sentiments.

Chapter 8: The Fiasco In The Grand Opéra

The Grand Opéra referred to the Palais Garnier, where it used to be housed (now there is the functional Opéra Bastille; the former opera house has become a tourist attraction). During the Nazi occupation, the Germans transformed the building to accommodate Germany's presence. Nazi Swastika flags hung between the Corinthian columns, and Germany sent companies there to perform works by German composers. The Opéra thus promoted German culture and propaganda, although it also remained quintessentially French. The Palais Garnier Grand Opéra was one of Hitler's first stops when he arrived in Paris.

After the war, the French were ashamed of their women having consorted with German soldiers and embarrassed about the widespread so-called "horizontal collaboration" under the Vichy regime, the French regime that collaborated with its Nazi occupiers. Some 200,000 babies with German fathers were born to French mothers. A woman who dared reject a German officer, like the blonde does with Karlheinz, would most likely have received widespread approbation from her countrymen and women.

Chapter 9: A Torturous Hour In The Jardin du Luxembourg

The German poet and novelist Rainer Maria Rilke was one of my father's favorite authors; he mentions him at least three times in this book. Rilke also often came up in Karlheinz's letters to Fräulein Sobbe. The setting of one of Rilke's most famous poems, *The Carousel*, is the Jardin du Luxembourg, and the setting of another, *The Panther*, is the Jardin des Plantes, also mentioned in this chapter.

Chapter 10: Herrn Von Rastenberg's Model

Unfortunately, I could not find any information about this supposed German *Wehrmacht* swimming pool in Paris during World War II, which is portrayed here in such an intriguing way. It must have been an existing pool that was requisitioned from the city by the Germans.

The façade of the Théâtre de la Gaîté still exists, but it is now a digital arts and modern music center operated by the city of Paris, called La Gaîté Lyrique. When it was still a theatre, at least two operettas with music by composer Franz Lehár were performed there: *Le Pays du Sourire* (The Land of Smiles) and *Frasquita*, which Karlheinz and Michi saw. During the German occupation of World War II, someone looted the theatre and a large chandelier installed by the director disappeared.

Chapter 11: Zazous And The Seine Terrace In St. Germain

The Zazous were a youth subculture during World War II in France. Young people expressed their individuality by wearing big or garish clothing like that which Karlheinz describes, which was derived from the "zoot suit" fashion in America a few years before (popularized by the musician Cab Calloway). The male hairdo my father describes, long hair with a wave in the middle and the sides gelled and combed back to meet at the back of the head, was called a "quiff".

The French Vichy regime adopted a policy of cooperation and collaboration with its Nazi occupiers. It had an ultra-conservative morality and enacted repressive laws against the restless and disenchanted Zazous, who were trying to defy the forces of occupation and the austerity of the Vichy regime with their extravagant clothing and other customs.

Regarding the pervasive use of scarce cosmetics by French women during wartime, the use of bright red lipstick was a sometimes a conscious gesture of defiance by Allied women; Hitler apparently hated red lipstick.

The noted landscape architect and royal gardener, André Le Nôtre, laid out the Grande Terrasse, overlooking the Seine Valley in the Paris suburb of Saint-Germain-en-Laye, between 1668 and 1675. It is part of the royal gardens of the Chateau de Saint Germain. The terrace is only one and a half miles long, but looks much longer because of its design. It is absolutely beautiful, with stunning views.

Karlheinz and Michi's relationship has entered a new, more serious stage. Moving from the formal address "*Sie*" and "*Fräulein Michen/Herr Stöss*", to the more informal "*du*" and the use of each other's first names, symbolizes these deepening feelings towards each other. This division still exists today in Germany, and one switches from "*Sie*" to "*du*" with a new acquaintance either if given permission by the other person or by mutual consent. However, usage is much more fluid and variable nowadays.

Chapter 12: *The Rapist* In The Grand Guignol

Le Théâtre du Grand-Guignol was a unique small theatre from its opening in 1897 until it closed in 1962, in the Pigalle/Montmartre district of Paris. The name means "The Theatre of the Great Puppet" and it specialized in naturalistic horror shows with gruesomely realistic special effects, similar to today's "splatter" films. Today, the International Visual Theatre, a company that presents plays in sign language, occupies the building. A former chapel housed the old theatre; there were angels over the orchestra and the box seats Karlheinz mentions looked like former confessionals. It was the smallest theatrical venue in Paris, with only 293 seats. At the time of WWII, the theatre was focusing more on psychological drama than on gory horror; insanity was one of the theatre's favorite and recurring themes. Audiences waned in the years after WWII. Management attributed the audience decline and later the closing of the theatre to the fact that the actual horrors of the Holocaust eclipsed the simulated horrors shown on stage.

My husband commented that my father might have gone into such detail about the play he and Michi attended because he saw it as an allegory of the war. Let us suppose that is the case. It is difficult to say whether Karlheinz thought Germany was the frail-looking, disadvantaged blind man who gains the upper hand and triumphs, or the other way around: Germany was the presumed murderer, capable of turning his madness on and off, wrongly convinced that he could easily outwit a feeble old blind man.

Chapter 13: The Reformation Day Celebration

The church this chapter takes place in is the *Christuskirche*, the German Protestant Church of Paris. Founded in 1894 as a

Lutheran church for the German community, it is today a United Church, a church formed from the merger of two or more different Protestant Christian denominations.

Karlheinz refers to the "expatriate Germans" as distinct from the soldiers and communication assistants. Presumably these were German citizens who were in Paris for non-military reasons and lived and worked there. The vast majority of Germans belonged to a Christian church during the Nazi era, overwhelmingly either the German Evangelical Church (Lutheran) or the Roman Catholic Church. The leaders of both churches made many compromises with Nazi authorities and were outwardly supportive of Nazi measures.

Chapter 14: Tears Fall In My Heart

The *Inconnue de la Seine* (The Unknown Woman of the Seine) was an unidentified young woman whose supposed death mask became popular after the body of a young woman was pulled out of the River Seine at the Quai du Louvre in Paris around the late 1880s. The body showed no signs of violence, so the authorities suspected suicide. Apparently a pathologist at the Paris Morgue cast a wax plaster death mask of her face, although there were disputes whether this was indeed the young woman's face. They never discovered the true identity of the girl. We actually had a plaster copy of this mask hanging in our childhood home and I now have it on the wall of my current home.

•   •   •

I was incredibly sad as I read the last words of the book, profoundly touched by the melancholy of it all. Like I said, my father and Michi stayed in touch for years after the war, and my mother met her as well. When I asked my mother some questions about Michi, she said that my father had stayed in touch with most of his old girlfriends and that she had met several of them. There are envelopes full of pictures from wartime and afterwards, with a different woman's name on each envelope. My mother patiently assembled the envelopes following my father's death. She told me it took her weeks. I find it remarkable that she knew who all those women were and could identify them by name on sight.

· · ·

It is worth talking about the poems and lyrics included in this manuscript. I used "accepted" translations from the Internet whenever I could. Of course, this avenue was not open to my father. I wonder if he had books for the song lyrics and poems he quotes, but I suspect that most, or even all, came from his memory, because this was an ability he showed throughout the rest of his life.

Young people, especially in Germany and in Europe overall, seem to have been much better educated than Americans. Germany used a "classical" approach to education, which is a structured, rigorous, history-based, idea-oriented educational model that exposes students to the great minds of the past through literature, essays, and philosophy. Memorization was a big part of the German school curriculum and young people at the time could easily spout famous poetry, lyrics and text excerpts. My father's erudite sophistication at such a young age continually amazed me.

The modern German school system has undoubtedly changed since then, but the fact remains that the education received in a *Gymnasium*, the highest level of high school education in Germany resulting in an *Abitur* diploma, is equivalent to about two years of college in the United States. That is why American college students attend study abroad programs in their junior year, when their high school diploma is then worth the same as that of most European countries.

・ ・ ・

It is interesting to me that my father spends quite a lot of time musing about war and peace and his yearning for the latter, and does not at all seem like the "occupier" of a country. I would like to take a moment to reflect on my father's expressed desire for peace. Even during wartime, Karlheinz seems to have had a continual yearning for peace. My mother always said that he did not discriminate against any group of people and was a live-and-let-live kind of person. I agree with this assessment; my father would criticize individuals but not peoples. Literature, music, art and culture were so important to him, he would condemn war as destructive on this basis alone, not to mention the loss of life. The bombing of Dresden and the destruction of other cultural European capitals devastated him, as did what he saw as the needless deaths of so many young men (an entire generation) along with civilians.

He obviously counts himself very lucky to live for a time in Paris, a lifelong dream of his, and he open-heartedly embraces that beautiful city's many musical, cultural and historical offerings. I mentioned earlier that *The Book of Michi* is as much a travelogue of Parisian sites as a love story. My father kept a lifelong love of France (he was a Francophile of the highest order) and a transfer there with his family in 1968 thrilled him. The Burroughs Corporation transferred him to Paris from Detroit, Michigan, where we were then living. This was before business executives clamored for overseas assignments, and my father received "hardship pay" for being willing to move with his family to Paris.

I therefore lived in Paris from the time I was 11 years old until I was 18 and went away to college at Georgetown University in Washington, DC. Even though I attended the American School of Paris, I learned to speak French fluently, which has served me well throughout the rest of my life, and I eventually became as enamored of France as my father. I didn't like it when we first moved there when I was 11, but I succumbed to its charms by the time I was around 16.

As a family, we visited many of the sites mentioned in this book. We walked on the Seine Terrace in St. Germain, and I have pictures of my sister and me riding ponies with our cousins in the Jardin du Luxembourg. We visited many of the Loire Valley castles, and this is where my husband and I went on our honeymoon when we were married in 1984. I also briefly lived in the Montmartre neighborhood when I returned to Paris for a year and a half after college, and got to know this rich historic neighborhood well.

• • •

My father's book made me reflect further on his spirituality. Coming from the East, my father was Lutheran, and my mother, coming from Bavaria, was Roman Catholic. Germans were religiously segregated along geographical lines. My parents' marriage had a whiff of scandal about it, being considered a "mixed marriage". Irene's father insisted Karlheinz respect Irene's faith and agree to raise any children that resulted from the marriage as Catholic, which is what happened, as that was also an American Catholic Church requirement. My mother, sister and I went to Catholic Mass every Sunday; my father did not join us, nor did he attend Lutheran services.

The major differences between the two religions are that Catholics believe in a faith that is formed by life and work, and that one can achieve salvation in this manner, whereas Lutherans believe that showing love and faith to Jesus Christ will bring them salvation. Also, Catholics place doctrinal authority in the Pope, the traditions of the church and the Scriptures. Lutherans believe that only the Holy Scriptures hold authority in determining church doctrine. In Germany, geographic lines divided the country by religion; where you came from, usually determined what religion you were.

I never thought of my father as particularly religious, although I would not describe him as an atheist. I now see through his books and letters that he did indeed believe in God, and that spirituality was apparently much more a part of his life when he was young, before he married and had children.

• • •

Eingesperrt! Bilder aus einer seelischen und aus einer körperlichen Gefangenschaft (Locked Up! Images From An Emotional And A Physical Imprisonment) was the second book Karlheinz wrote, between December 1947 and April 1948, when he was back in Germany with his refugee mother and sister. He was 27 years old at the time. It recounts his wartime and prison camp experiences, including his capture by the Allied Forces. It consists of two parts, *Part 1: The Scylla Of The Uniform* and *Part 2: The Charybdis Of The Barbed Wire*.

The mythical sea monsters of Greek mythology inspired the titles of the two parts. Scylla and Charybdis were located across from each other, and each posed a different, undesirable danger to sailors navigating between them. Our idioms for this type of situation are "the lesser of two evils", "on the horns of a dilemma", "between the devil and the deep blue sea", "between a rock and a hard place", etc. Choosing between two equally dangerous extremes leads unavoidably to disaster.

Karlheinz wrote *Locked Up!* by hand on the backs of American Army requisition forms. Paper was in short supply after the war, and I originally thought my father got the forms from his sister Ilse, who worked for the American military command that controlled the city of Rehau, where what remained of the family had resettled. I recently found out through a resume I found among his papers that he had worked there as well, as a clerk, translator and court interpreter for the U.S. military. It was most likely the only paper he could get his hands on. Maybe he was at loose ends when he returned to Germany and had ample time to write about his recent experiences while pondering his next steps.

At just 18 years of age, Karlheinz's sister Ilse married her boss at the American military command and moved with him to the town of Lucketts, Virginia, a farming community a short distance from Washington, DC, after first living for a while in New Jersey. Her mother Else followed, living in a trailer on Ilse's husband's farm and learning English, becoming a licensed practical nurse, getting a driver's license, and taking up painting as a hobby, all in her late 50s and 60s. She serves as a constant inspiration to me.

•   •   •

I was feeling a sense of excitement as I took hold of the faded handwritten pages in the tattered envelope. This book was nothing like *Michi*: it was more of a draft, with crossed-out parts and inserted words, and the writing was very faint. I realized I would have to decipher and type each word one by one, in order to even read the manuscript.

What a revelation—it constantly amazed me what a wonderful writer my father was. I still couldn't believe that I was the first person to have read these books in over 70 years. A few of the corrections and revisions seemed to be in a different handwriting. Had someone helped him edit his manuscript? Had he ever thought of submitting it for publication? Did he have plans to write a third book? Did he see himself as a writer? These were all questions for which there were no answers. My mother confirmed that she had never read either book, although she was well aware of their existence.

I looked forward to my deciphering sessions—to finding out what happened next—even though it was rough going, especially dealing with the technical terms. But I now had a much fuller picture of my father's wartime experiences, and the anecdotes I had been told as a child fell into place along the timeline inside my head.

The complete text of *Locked Up!* follows, and again, I have some notes on the text at the end of each part. An introduction precedes *Part 1: The Scylla Of The Uniform*, followed by untitled chapters 1 through 16. *Part 2: The Charybdis Of The Barbed Wire* has titled chapters 1 through 10, followed by an afterword.

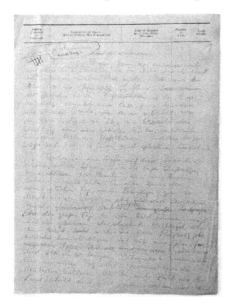 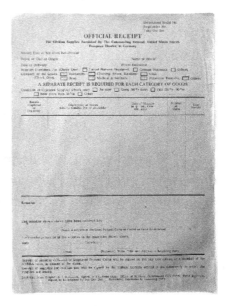

Locked Up! Was written on the backs of
US Army requisition forms, 1947-48

LOCKED UP!
Images From An Emotional And A Physical Imprisonment

Karlheinz Stöss

Written December 1947 – April 1948

(Translated by Helga Warren)

Part 1: The Scylla of the Uniform

Introduction

From an airplane, one has a clear overview of the wide, flat landscape. There in the west is Cherbourg, visible as a huge dark spot on the coast, and in the east lies Le Havre as counterpoint. Between the two coastal cities, at the mouth of the Orne River, one can make out Caen, a beautiful, old city embodying all the characteristics of Normandy: a bewitching harmony of Gothic churches, enchanted castles, blooming apple trees and the eternal scent of pommes frites and fried lake fish.

As we drift down closer to this city, we can make out the narrow streets, where the people, small as ants, scurry back and forth. They rush through the summery day running errands, or to work, or to amuse themselves, or to do a host of things. But all think often of the big day that must soon come, and that circles over them like a hunting bird of prey, like our plane, but which soon will come plummeting down to strike its target and unleash fresh horrors upon them. "Débarquement" (Disembarkation), is what the French call this day, and "Invasion" is what the German soldiers say, deployed across the landscape in large numbers, waiting, waiting for the hour in which alarm sirens will cry forth along the entire Normandy coast.

Out of a narrow house in Caen, with ground level windows thickly hung with curtains, a young German officer strode forth. Pleased with himself, he bounced along in his soft made-to-measure leather boots, as he took off his thin leather gloves and his driver, Gefreiter (acting corporal) Krause, quickly and deferentially opened the car door with a sharp click of his heels.

The Oberleutnant (first lieutenant) of the Luftnachrichtentruppe (air force communications service), Dr. Egon Dietershagen, stepped into the car and stretched out contentedly on the blue leather seats. After Krause had slammed the door and started the Mercedes, the Oberleutnant carefully wiped the lipstick remaining on his lips from Odette. "Oh, that little black devil!" he thought to himself in sleepy satisfaction. "How many thousands of francs has she already cost me? But it's worth it, by God, it's worth it! The fire this graceful little animal with the rough voice has!" He felt like Tannhäuser on Mount Venus every time he was in her boudoir, filled with sweet oriental scents. This day needed a worthy ending.

"Krause!" he shouted good-naturedly to the front of the car. "Krause, see to it I'm served a nice Burgundy tonight. Unteroffizier (sergeant) Sammler should make us some omelets and prepare a platter of oysters. Tell Fahnenjunkerfeldwebel (NCO cadet sergeant) Gast and Fähnrich (NCO cadet) Mein, who usually dine with me, that tonight they should make an exception and eat with the rest of the company."

"Jawohl, Herr Oberleutnant!" answered Krause, as he raced the car over the road toward the coastal military base "Golden Pheasant".

Dietershagen thought about his company. How well everything had worked out! When the air force communications service started monitoring flight notifications about two years ago with ultra-short waves and set up an organization for this purpose, he had volunteered for this new service. What an intelligent and farsighted decision this had turned out to be! This way he could stay in the beautiful French countryside, where he had now been for over three years. He lived comfortably, and as company commander of the technology apparatus position, which simultaneously served as one of the most important bases in the coastal defense system, he exercised the power of a minor king.

Soon the five radars of the "Goldfasan" (Golden Pheasant) Company radar detection station came into view: two Würzburg-Riesen short-range radars with their huge round reflecting mirrors, two Freya-Geräte medium-range radars, whose steel structures stretched straight up in the mild air, and a Wassermann long-range detection radar with a 50-meter tall tower. "Damn it", thought Oberleutnant Dietershagen, "somebody shot it up again today." Twisted and mangled, the steel pipes at the topmost part of the tower stuck out at odd angles, and the transformers that hung between them were bent and shattered. "Disgusting, a damned shame," he murmured. "The Wassermann radar is hardly ever operational. As soon as it's fixed, it's shot up again by these ever-present British fighter-bombers. I wonder what happened this time."

At the entrance of the station, between the barbed wire barriers, Fahnenjunkerfeldwebel Gast was already standing there to greet his superior officer. With measured steps, he approached the car, saluted with a stoic face, and reported in icy tones: "At 16:30 enemy fighter planes again shot at the Wassermann. Despite our flak fire, roughly 20 shots on the Wassermann met their target. Obergefreiter (corporal) Rupprecht was killed under this fire. He suffered a hard death, Herr Oberleutnant: a shot under the eye. His wound unspeakably tormented him for half an hour before he died."

A few beads of sweat had appeared on Dietershagen's brow. He was going to have to draft another long report to the regiment. The musicians' train would have to be ordered from Lisieux for the funeral, and also he would have to order the construction brigade to start immediately on the reconstruction of the Wassermann. "What stupidity!" thought the first lieutenant to himself, "Now I won't get any Burgundy or oysters today. What a shame." And he had so wished for that desired outcome to this day and not any other.

"Gast," he said somewhat nervously, "report with Kuklinski and Von Schütz to me in about an hour. Then we'll quickly take care of what is required."

As the Mercedes drove away to the officers' barracks, Feldwebel Gast slowly walked back to the analysis bunker. This was his domain. Here, he functioned as the platoon commander of the analysis progression. Radar detection data was analyzed on a large layout map and transmitted to the anti-aircraft and flak services as grid coordinates.

Gast had occupied this post for about three months, but it was not a trivial matter to carry out his duties competently. He was constantly at odds with Dietershagen. Just yesterday, they had had a huge confrontation. Gast had not gone to the analysis bunker at any point during the morning, as he knew that the relief group was in expert hands under the competent direction of Obergefreiter (corporal) Bergmann, whom he could totally rely upon. However, when Dietershagen turned up for his inspection, the soldiers had just detected ship targets on the radar, which, under the effects of the invasion psychosis that had gripped the company, threw Dietershagen into the greatest disarray. "Where is the platoon leader?" he had screamed. Although Bergmann had called Erhard Gast immediately, the latter only appeared a quarter of an hour later. The commander's patience was not up to such a long wait. In the meantime, he had left the analysis bunker to climb up into the observation cockpit of one of the revolving Freya medium-range radars, to take a turn himself, watching the ships' progression on the cathode-ray tube. This is where Gast telephoned him as soon as he had arrived at the analysis bunker. That's when Dietershagen started screaming at him with uncontrolled rage, raging on for about ten minutes about his complete incompetence and lack of interest in his job. As Gast almost collided with the commander on the narrow bunker steps after this monumental chewing-out, which the commander thought had irredeemably brought him down, Gast showed no signs of depression. He had a long, smoking cigar in his mouth and was walking the base dog Orpheus on a leash, which was strongly disapproved of; his mood seemed to be quite excellent as he made a show of taking the cigar out of his mouth and bringing his hand up to the brim of his hat in a nonchalant salute. "You're now smoking cigars?" was the commander's muttered question. "In fact, I am," was the grinning platoon commander's reply, "and it suits me admirably!" Once again, he had triumphed over his commanding lieutenant. In that moment, however, this lieutenant vowed he would finally, somehow definitively, show him what a chopping block was for. But Gast had long known he had it out for him and had armed himself for battle.

As Erhard Gast arrived at the entrance to the bunker, Sergeant Major Von Schütz was just climbing the stairs and taking deep breaths of the fresh air. He was like NCO Sergeant Major Gast, only perhaps a little more sensitive, and greatly over-civilized. Both were twenty-four-year-old students. Gast studied philosophy and Von Schütz studied music. Because of their status as soul mates, and because of a shared unfitness for service in the Prussian military structure, they had made a sort of protection and support pact with each other to provide the other with aid in the face of constant attacks from the notorious "Prussians" of the company.

Although Gast had risen to the rank of officer cadet, because of his unwillingness to deliver the required slavish obedience, he had been the longest-serving NCO officer cadet in the regiment for quite some time, unable to count on a promotion to lieutenant. He refused to address officers in the 3rd person singular as required, despite Dietershagen's continued reproaches. As justification, he referenced a direct order from the Reichsmarschall (General of the Armies) explicitly forbidding the use of the 3rd person address. The boss made it clear to him, however, that the regiment commander would never elevate someone to the officer corps who persisted in addressing him or another officer as "Sie" (formal "you") despite the support of the command from on high. So Erhard Gast stayed stubbornly stuck at the threshold of the officer corps...

5.

Things were a little different for Ulrich Von Schütz. Although he had already progressed to the officer cadet rank, he had been stripped of this recognition before the year was out, as he was guilty of a failure to carry out orders during his officer-training course. However, his offense was of such an honorable and admirable nature that Erhard considered him a dear and like-minded friend for this alone.

Sometimes, if he was in a congenial group, Ulrich Von Schütz would tell the story of the event that catapulted him back into the lowliest ranks of the military. This is how it happened. Their superiors sent the group of officers in training outside one Sunday. In small, relaxed groupings the students wandered along the rural road talking amongst themselves, when the sole lieutenant in charge suddenly turned to his subordinates and called out to them sharply: "We will now conduct an obedience exercise. Up ahead, there is a dog coming towards us. As soon as he passes you, you will give him a perfect salute. Six steps before and two steps after, most precisely. Whoever cannot follow this order," he continued icily, "can pack his things tomorrow and return to his troop, because the soldier in question will have proved with his unwillingness that he is incapable of unquestioningly carrying out orders, and is therefore totally unsuited to being a dutiful officer."

Following this chilling address, which more or less caused the blood to freeze in the men's veins, the afore-mentioned mutt came crookedly trotting towards the soldiers. Since little time for reflection remained and the lieutenant had already cried out a thundering "Go!" to the first in line, the soldiers sharply snapped their hands to the brims of their hats, one after the other. They stretched the fingers of their left hands taut and all eyes rested earnestly on the nonchalantly approaching cur during this display of "honor".

Every soldier, except for a single man, carried out the ordered salute. This lone holdout was Ulrich Von Schütz. Instead of bringing his hand to the brim of his hat, he angrily stuck his balled fist in his pocket and spit audibly several times in a fit of rage and disgust. As if stung by a tarantula, the lieutenant flew towards him, screamed at him for several minutes, and let him know in no uncertain terms that he was henceforth summarily dismissed from the officer-training course. The very next day, they sent Ulrich back to his regiment. In his evaluation, stood: "Feldwebel Von Schütz had to be stripped of his NCO officer cadet status because of his refusal to carry out a legitimate order. He has showed conduct unbecoming of a soldier, which has led to him being definitively excluded from any further officer training." It was in this manner that they turned Ulrich Von Schütz away at the threshold of the officer corps...

6.

Erhard Gast said to Ulrich: "Hey, we're supposed to go see the boss to talk about what happened today. He just went back to his 'residence'. I could tell he was upset when I told him about Ruprecht's death. It seems to have cast a pall over his gallant adventures in Caen."

"Hmm," Ulrich Von Schütz said thoughtfully, "so we've got to go see the Prussian academic. By the way, have you noticed that university graduates are often much worse sticklers for the rules, than are those who heaved themselves up through the ranks to the status of officers through decades of obstinate yelling at subordinates and excessive displays of submission to higher-ups?"

"You're right, Ulrich", said Erhard, nodding his assent as they slowly made their way to the officers' barracks. "But it doesn't seem to me that Dietershagen will ever make it to the elite military ruling class, because he's a vengeful, back-stabbing coward. If he decides he doesn't like you, you'll never be free of his retaliation and drama. Well, we both know what we're talking about."

"Yeah, Erhard, you're so right," Ulrich Von Schütz interjected. "I'm just wondering if he has it out for me because of the brilliant advice I gave Rübsam during the haircut inspection. Kuklinski, that snitch, probably couldn't wait to tell him all about it."

"Uh oh, Ulrich, what did you do now?" laughed Erhard.

"You know that Corporal Rübsam always has a perfect Prussian haircut, matchstick-long, with ugly, shaved sides. At the haircut inspection this morning, I advised him to let his hair grow nice and long for a change, loudly enough so that Kuklinski, who was inspecting a different row, was sure to hear. I pointed to my concert-pianist mane, which has given me no end of trouble in all my postings, and suggested he use my haircut as a model for his own. First, there was dead silence, but then everyone started grinning and snickering. Kuklinski was mad as a wet hen that a non-Prussian like myself had upended the entire company. Rübsam just stared at me, as if struck by lightning."

The two friends howled with laughter at this bit of fun. At that moment, they saw NCO Sergeant Major Kuklinski coming towards them, also on his way to meet with the boss. The two adversarial parties greeted each other with a feigned friendliness. Stupi—that's what his fellow soldiers called him because of his profound lack of intellect—was fairly wound- up. This was actually always the case when he knew he was to a have a face-to-face with the boss. This time he could not hide a quite different reason for his excitement. With studied nonchalance he said: "Today we had the most enemy flight activity that we have had in months. The backcountry from St. Lô to Rouen and all the way to Amiens, and also the Paris area, were heavily bombed. Tomorrow it might be the coast's turn. And we probably only have a few days until the Invasion takes place. Damnable situation! I think we have a lot of unpleasantness ahead of us!"

"Of course, Max," the two students agreed, "just see to it you smuggle your Raymonde onto the base, otherwise you're going to be really unhappy during the occupation."

"No, I'd better not," Stupi demurred. "I think we won't feel like doing that kind of thing by then."

With this, they had arrived at the boss's barracks. His servant Lisette was just leaving his quarters with a basket full of empty Champagne bottles.

■　　■　　■

After the boss had given his instructions to the three sergeant majors in a tired tone of voice, he added that as of tomorrow, nobody was to leave the military base. Starting June 6th, all had to be in a state of military readiness, as several indicators pointed unmistakably to a coming invasion.

As the three turned to exit, the boss called out after them: "Oh, I almost forgot. I still have a bone to pick with you, Von Schütz. What on earth were you thinking, when you advised Rübsam this morning to…"

Kuklinski and Gast could no longer hear anything as they returned to their quarters with vastly different interpretations of the tongue-lashing that was even now taking place.

7.

At dinner, Ulrich Von Schütz told his friend Gast about how the boss had reproached him. It had been incendiary. "If you had not already been relieved of your officer training status, I would have ripped it from you right now!" the boss had railed. "People like you ruin my entire company!" "Why can't we tell him he ruins the souls of his underlings?" Ulrich asked querulously. "I would love to do that, but I don't want to go in front of the war tribunal, so close to when all hell breaks loose."

"You're right, my dear Ulrich," said Erhard Gast. "That kind of courage costs one too much. Let's forget the whole sorry mess tonight, because as of tomorrow we have to stand at the ready for the sound of the alarm. Let's go out tonight and do it up right. I can rely on Bergmann, who's taking the night shift tonight. Will you come with me to see old Jérôme at the 'Bar Américain' in Luc-sur-Mer? We'll tie one on before everything goes to hell in a handbasket."

"Oh, that's a great idea," cheered Ulrich. "Luc, here we come; I can't wait!"

As the two decidedly out-of-the-ordinary Luftwaffe sergeant majors were leaving the "Golden Pheasant" military base, dusk was just settling on the flat coastland, like a gently fluttering scarf. Delicate pastels colored the sky in the west, colors like those that Millet, the painter of Normandy, had captured so perfectly in his masterwork "L'Angelus". Unfortunately, Erhard Gast and Ulrich Von Schütz had their evening reverie rudely interrupted behind the radar station on the road to Luc, as they suddenly came upon Oberfeldwebel (master sergeant) Kuklinski acting out his sadistic, diabolical plan as tonight's leader of the bicycle patrol. For weeks, he had admonished the weak and thoroughly intimidated Obergefreiter (corporal) Bingelmann to learn at last how to ride a bicycle. Being the only non-bicycle-rider in the company, no one could ever assign him to the nightly bicycle patrols. Because of his unfortunate and unusual ungainliness, Bingelmann, a street sweeper by profession, had never learned how to ride a bike. At lunch, Kuklinski had informed him he would be called upon for that evening's bicycle patrol, and that he, Kuklinski, would teach him himself one hour before the patrol was to start. Here on the road he had been torturing poor Bingelmann for quite some time, and the latter, bleeding and scraped up, was just being hoisted onto his bike again by two NCOs. "Push!" screamed Kuklinski, and amid loud laughter, his fellow bicycle patrol participants gave the profusely sweating Bingelmann a hefty push. "Let go!" ordered Kuklinski shortly thereafter, his coarse features distorted by a nasty grin. The two accomplices gave another shove and then stepped away to either side. The terrified Bingelmann perched on his seat like an ape as the bike wobbled perilously back and forth. He could somehow propel himself forward a few feet before he teetered on the edge of the roadside ditch, his bicycle tilting sharply, and tumbled off, head over heels. As Kuklinski slapped his thigh in delight, hooting with laughter, many of Bingelmann's comrades joining in, the poor, tormented enlisted man crawled out of the ditch, face flaming red, bathed in sweat, with trembling knees.

"You're making astounding progress!" roared Kuklinski, "I think we're ready to go! Hang your weapon around your neck, Bingelmann, and lead the line." But as the latter just stood there with bowed head, not reacting even a little, the head sergeant major screamed again, his voice crackling with rage: "Move it, you wet blanket, didn't you hear what I just said? Grab your weapon, and up on the beast!" At this, Bingelmann turned towards his machine gun to hang it around his neck as ordered. Only when he already had his hand on the gun did Kuklinski mercifully put an end to his gruesome game, calling out: "Just leave it, you loser, and go to bed. But you'd better learn how to ride a bike by next week, or I'll give you another lesson, and it won't be an easy one like tonight..."

9.

By the time Gast and Von Schütz arrived at the seaside town of Luc-sur-Mer after a short walk on the road that hugged the coastline, darkness had descended. The moon shone brightly and cast a ghostly cold, white light on the minefields and the concrete obstacles on the flat, sandy beach.

Coastal fortifications like those shown in the weekly news shows were virtually non-existent between the cities of Cherbourg and Le Havre. Here and there, the infantry had built a small fortification directly at the water's edge, but kilometer-long stretches had no fortifications at all; at most there was an illusory minefield or arrangement of "Rommelspargel" ("Rommel asparagus").

When Erhard Gast explained to his parents and relatives during his last vacation what this famous "Atlantic Wall" really looked like, no one wanted to believe him. One of his uncles, a drinking-game champion, even declared: "You just haven't noticed that the facades of the houses on the coast road are just for show. When you hydraulically lower them, huge coastal fortifications suddenly appear…"

"Oh, my dear Uncle Erwin. You should come to the coast sometime. Wouldn't it surprise you to see what the Atlantic Wall really looks like!" thought Erhard Gast to himself, simply smiling and shaking his head.

The "Bar Américain", presided over by old Jérôme, lay directly on the beach promenade. When one stepped out the door and crossed the street, one was standing right at the water's edge and could see all the way to where the ocean and the sky met at the horizon. A few meters from the coastline were iron fortifications anchored far apart from each other, designed to deter the approach of enemy landing craft.

Erhard and Ulrich entered the bar amid happy jubilation. The French, mostly from Luc's better social circles, sat at small tables drinking Champagne, aperitifs, Cointreau, Cognac, or various cocktails. No German soldiers were here tonight, as the infantrymen and military engineers had not had permission to leave the military bases for several weeks now. The two German visitors were no strangers to the bar regulars or to the bartender, Jérôme. In fact, they seemed to be remarkably popular, as a friendly "Bonsoir" or "Allo" rang out from several tables. Ulrich, who felt completely at home here, nodded to everyone in a chummy manner and confidently strode to the bar, where he and Erhard sat down on high stools and ordered two double Cognacs to start with. As he shook the cocktail shaker, Jérôme looked at the two regulars thoughtfully and asked if there was indeed a possibility that the "Débarquement" (Landing) could take place as early as tonight. The two friends looked at each other, somewhat taken aback. "Sure," Ulrich replied, who, like Erhard, spoke good French, "that's certainly possible. We think it will take a few more days, though." The cocktail-shaking Jérôme stared at them unusually hard and pointed through the door, which an entering customer had just opened, to the metal obstacles that lay outside in the moonlight, washed over by the surging ocean, and said somewhat hesitantly: "The British and Americans will easily be able to land here. Look at these sorry metal barriers;

you can't keep your enemy at bay with that... that's nothing, nothing at all."

This was not news to the two sergeant majors; they already knew, and were just waiting resignedly for the coming catastrophe to arrive. After they had washed down a few cocktails, sunk deep in thought, they slowly got caught up in the damp festivities that surrounded them; they started chatting with their French friends and several of the patrons eventually persuaded Ulrich Von Schütz to play dance tunes on the piano. His specialties were jazz, swing and jive in all their variations. He was especially good at Anglo-American evergreens, which he masterfully played in a swinging, syncopated rhythm that more or less brought the dancing couples to a state of ecstasy almost as soon as he started. He was well aware of his musical gift and always enjoyed the fervor and passion he could awaken through his playing. Erhard Gast sat down at the drums, and with gentle rhythm and pealing melody, the two launched into "Smoke Gets in Your Eyes."

Obergefreiter (corporal) Hans Bergmann, who was sitting in the analysis bunker of the "Golden Pheasant" base at the command table, glanced down at his wristwatch; it was almost 11:00 pm. Strange how quiet it was outside today. No radar had intercepted any target; the coastal watch was also quiet and had reported no enemy flight sorties. The soldiers on the night watch sat sleepily at their posts, dozing off occasionally. "Working in the analysis platoon of Feldwebel Gast is actually a plum assignment," thought Post Inspector Bergmann to himself. "This young student at least respects his elders, is not at all arrogant, and is unfailingly helpful. How much worse my colleagues in the radar platoon of Oberfeldwebel Kuklinski have it, a difference like day and night!" How good it was, the thought came to him, that he had told his platoon commander Gast, the last time he had had night duty, about what had happened at the regimental headquarters in Falaise, which had led to his forced transfer up here to the "Front". His assignment there was to type up letters dictated to him by the aide-de-camp or the regimental secretary. One day, fate caught up with him. Because he was so good at spelling and grammar, he rarely made any sort of mistake. It was for this reason that it surprised him one day that the regimental secretary handed him back a letter in which the aide-de-camp had underlined in red the lowercase "b" of the term "in bezug" (regarding). "Type this again, but this time with a capital B," ordered the regimental secretary.

"No, no, Herr Oberfeld, please, here, see for yourself," was his reply, "check in the Duden (German grammar reference book): you spell 'in bezug' with a lowercase b!" Once he had erased the red underlining, the regimental secretary duly returned with the letter to the aide-de-camp. "I already returned this mistyped crap once!" the aide-de-camp roared. "I will sign nothing that's wrong!" "But Captain, I checked it myself in the Duden: you spell 'in bezug' with a lower-case 'b'; Bergmann is right," was the secretary's sober reply. "Damn it," the captain yelled, "I insist that this disobedient fellow write 'in bezug' like every sensible person would, namely with an uppercase 'B'. I couldn't care less what it says in the Duden!" Upon receiving this clarification, Bergmann did something monstrous: he simply could not carry out the order to write "in bezug" wrong; he just couldn't bring himself to do it. The consequence of this insubordination and failure to carry out a direct order was his forced transfer to the "Golden Pheasant" coastal military base.

When he told this story to his new superior, Gast was furious with the "complete idiots", as he called them, at the regimental headquarters. Ever since then, Gast had treated him with exceptional warmth and friendliness. In Gast, Bergmann had come face-to-face with a true human being instead of a military automaton. How welcome that was to this longtime subversive! There was no shortage of ignoramuses decorated with cords and stars who took out their bad moods on the poor "Scheuerfrauen (scrubwomen) of the Wehrmacht". But once in a while there was someone like Sergeant Major Gast, upstanding and good. "Without rays of sunshine like this in the regiment's general pigsty, it would be much more difficult to be here, even unbearable," thought Hans Bergmann to himself, with an unusual mix of bitterness and quiet glee.

But whenever Bergmann thought they had broken his spirit for good, there was always an unfailing pick-me-up: the thought of his wife Monika in Heidelberg. She was a source of never-ending joy and inner happiness. Women like his Monika were rare. With a smile, he pulled his wallet out of his uniform, opened it, and took out the picture of the young, laughing woman with her dark hair parted in the middle. How impishly she smiled at him! These damn vacation bans! Because of them, he had not seen his Monika for 14 months. If only he could return home soon! But this ridiculous invasion still stood before him. And soon, soon the time would come...

12.

The two radar operators suddenly stood up from their observation of the huge glass map, readjusted their headphones, and, with their many instruments, recorded the courses of the enemy aircraft that they had picked up on the radar near the English coast. Right after that, the marine observation posts began reporting ship targets approaching the coast. As per regulations, Bergmann called the boss and informed him of the situation. Soon several radar operators were reporting huge flights of enemy bombers and several ship targets on the cathode-ray tubes, in between Cherbourg and Le Havre. Coastal defense, flak, infantry, fog-spreaders, anti-aircraft and special forces were all mobilized; soon after, that long-awaited proclamation, one almost of relief, streamed out of every telex machine, screeched out of all the telephones, screamed out from thousands of sirens: "Invasion… invasion!!!"

13.

Shortly after 11:00 pm old Jérôme had locked the door to the bar so that no light would shine out if someone opened it. For some time now, there had been uninterrupted droning in the sky, bombs falling in the distance, and flak from some of the nearby bases hammering away. The patrons of the "Bar Américain" remained undisturbed, however. The drinks had been flowing liberally for quite a while. Ulrich, who was at the piano, and Erhard, who was on the drums, had only to reach for the delectable drinks of all kinds that were constantly being proffered and to drain them; their fingers got looser and looser, and soon they were playing as if possessed. "Come on and hear, come on and hear Alexander's Ragtime Band," the two sang and played, while the French couples excitedly danced a wild, jumping swing.

In the brief pauses between foxtrots, the two friends heard the droning of airplanes and the hammering of flak. "Maybe already today…?" thought the friends as one, their eyes meeting thoughtfully. "So what!" proclaimed Ulrich Von Schütz, downing the rest of his cocktail in one gulp. "Let's play one more. Erhard, I suggest 'Symphonie', that beautiful French slow foxtrot that's supposedly the song by which the French Underground recognizes each other. Let's see what effect it will have right now."

Erhard Gast nodded in enthusiastic agreement, swept his brush over the drums, and started singing with deep feeling, as Ulrich made the tender rhythms of that bewitching song come alive:

Symphonie, symphonie d'un jour,
Qui chante toujours
Dans mon coeur lourd…
Et les mots et le son de ta voix
Maintenant je les retrouve en moi

C'est fini, c'est fini
Et j'...
(Symphony, symphony of a day,
Still singing
In my heavy heart...
And the words and the sound of your voice
Now I find them within myself
It's over, it's over
And I...)

"Yes, yes, it's over, it's over!" old Jérôme cried out suddenly, gesturing wildly with his arms as he stepped out from behind the bar. Shocked, Ulrich and Erhard stopped playing and singing; the dancers stood still in surprise, staring at the red-faced Jérôme, who excitedly proclaimed, "Ladies and gentlemen, the Landing has begun!" At this, the French broke out in celebratory cries. The hugging, kissing and yelling went on for some time, until someone suddenly started spontaneously singing the "Marseillaise", eagerly and unrestrainedly joined by all those present. Erhard and Ulrich, who had stood up at the first strains of the French national anthem, were as still as if struck by lightning. Suddenly sober, they started frantically wondering how they could quickly get out of there. Then Erhard whispered to Ulrich: "Let's go!" and they raced towards the exit. Jérôme, who had suddenly whipped out a pistol from behind the counter, barred their way with his weapon drawn, instructing them they should now consider themselves his prisoners. Erhard suddenly had an idea. He put his hand protectively on old Jérôme's shoulder and exclaimed: "Dear friend, we rejoice with you. But we've got to get going on our way now. Goodbye Jérôme, goodbye my friends!" With this, he gently but firmly pushed Jérôme out of the way, opened the door, and quickly stepped outside with Ulrich. The door slammed shut behind them; no one fired a shot.

Down at Base 45, landing ships had broken through the defensive cordon, and on the horizon, the two friends could see many warships and transport ships shining in the moonlight. Hand grenades crashed and machine gun fire crackled through the night.

"Will we make it back to the base, Erhard?" asked Ulrich as they crept along the coast road. "I think so," Erhard Gast answered. "See, the enemy could land on the coast at only a couple of spots so far. That means we'll be able to make it back to the base."

. . .

As they reported to Oberleutnant Dietershagen half an hour later, out of breath, the latter was sitting in military readiness, dressed in his steel helmet and leather overcoat, trying to look both martial and composed, yet succeeding at neither...

14.

As soon as the "Golden Pheasant" military base received the alarm signal that heralded the beginning of the Invasion, a plan, elaborated for years, took effect. No one seemed excited. In a relaxed way, totally calm, the various companies took their defense posts in the bunkers and the trenches, on the minefield, at the grenade launchers, and at the flak artillery stations.

Oberleutnant Dietershagen was not as calm as his 200 soldiers. How long would the base be able to resist? If he could actually pull off getting captured by the Americans or the British, as had long been his wont, all would be well. Undoubtedly, his upcoming captain's commission would follow him. If only he didn't get killed at the last minute through some stupid bit of bad luck! But he would be very careful. The command bunker was without a doubt the most secure on the entire base, and maybe he would not have to leave it at all before the surrender.

In the early dawn of the new day, the Allied troops that had landed between Cherbourg and Le Havre had already pushed past the mostly small defense camps to the front lines, along almost the entire coast. Even in the little woods that came right up to the "Golden Pheasant" base, there were already enemy tanks rolling towards their offensive positions. Infantry units dug holes from which to fire. Artillery observers sprang into action, and soon gunfire and shelling barraged the German position.

Outside, it was getting unbearable. Grenades even sometimes hit in the trenches, so that everyone outside of the bunker was in unrelenting danger. The companies, some of which had as yet been untried by warfare, accepted the situation with surprising calm. But not Dietershagen. Surrounded by staff officer observers, who constantly had to bring him updates about what was going on outside the bunker, he sat with trembling hands in front of the situation map. Soon, they started carrying the first wounded, and some dead, into the bunker. The sight of these seemed to make the first lieutenant sick to his stomach. In a low whisper, he asked his orderly where the bunker personnel were supposed to go to the bathroom, now that the latrine barracks were useless because of their location out in the open. "In a trench," he was told matter-of-factly. At this, he rose with apparent calm and hastened to the bunker exit. Since the northern sector had just sounded the tank alarm, a detachment was readying the antitank rocket launchers. Wide-eyed, Dietershagen stared into the serious, determined faces of the lance corporals.

Seeing that his boss was about to leave the bunker, a soldier pulled open the steel door. Hesitantly, Dietershagen stepped into the low-lying bunker forecourt. He heard the crack of grenades and the whistling gunfire that filled the surrounding air. The noise was thunderous, an incessant howling and pounding. Damn it, he had to take at least a few steps away from the bunker; he couldn't just drop his trousers here on the threshold. A grenade hit right by him; whistling splinters flew. This was too much for the leader of the company. Knock-kneed, he stumbled back inside the bunker, past men who were just leaving, armed to the teeth to resist the tanks, as ordered. He ran to his little bunker sleeping area, where he could grab an empty metal munitions box at the last minute, the very last minute...

The next day, he asked an announcer from the western sector how the gunfire was outside. "Awful, Sir," answered the man. "Fähnrich (officer candidate) Meier got hit right outside the bunker entrance. They blew his whole jaw off."

My God, the munitions boxes had to go out! For an hour, Dietershagen had tried to persuade himself to bring them out to the bunker entrance and fling them up from there. But then he saw Meier's bloody, torn face in his mind's eye, and made a different decision. He glanced around, looking for help. "Paulick," he called suddenly, "Paulick, come with me." Questioningly, the 19-year-old acting corporal followed him into his small bunker sleeping quarters. That there was an ungodly stench was the undeniable first impression. In the dim light of a bunker bulb, Paulick saw the munitions boxes and knew immediately what was about to happen. "Go a few steps away from the bunker entrance, Paulick, and throw the boxes out. But be careful that nothing happens to you. And you'd better go right away, because...". Instead of continuing, the boss held his nose silently. Before the young acting corporal bent over to pick up the boxes, he looked his boss right in the eye, so long, so forceful, and so full of contempt and disdain that the latter had to look away, helpless and defeated. As Paulick strode past Oberleutnant Dietershagen with the first two filled boxes, he stepped on his toe with the full weight of his combat boot. Dietershagen could not shake himself of the impression that he had done it on purpose.

16.

Because the personnel of the "Golden Pheasant" base had received the same strict orders that all German soldiers had received: to die rather than surrender, at noon on the third occupation day they deployed their tank forces and their few artillery forces against the many enemy Sherman tanks that were approaching their position in concentric formation. The commanders of the tanks had decided they would wipe out, once and for all, the last resisting German troops in this area. Fourteen men, who lost their lives for no reason at all a few minutes before the surrender, were the tribute that had to be paid in response to such idiotic orders.

A short while later, after American tank forces had successfully defeated the German base and herded together the resisting soldiers, a sigh of relief went up from both the victorious and the defeated. The Yankees distributed their cigarettes to the Germans, taking this opportunity to steal their wristwatches. Their commander, a major, stepped forward and directed his words to both the unshaven Germans and the olive-green-camouflage-faced Americans: "Thank God, boys, it's all over now".

Only once the German prisoners had readied themselves for their march in formation to the coast did Dietershagen come wobbling out of the bunker. All stared at him. He was wearing his elegant leather coat; in one hand he held a stuffed-full leather suitcase and in the other a Champagne bottle with two flutes. Somewhat self-consciously he stumbled over to the American major, set his suitcase down, brought his hand to the brim of his hat in a salute, and offering him a glass, asked him in broken English if he wouldn't like to make a toast to peace. After some hesitation, the American officer took the proffered glass and the German lieutenant poured Champagne for him first, then for himself. Immediately following the toast, Dietershagen emptied his glass with greedy gulps. Outraged, with clenched teeth, the ordinary soldiers of the two nations watched this embarrassing display. Obergefreiter Hans Bergmann had the fleeting thought that the bodies of those who had sacrificed their lives in the last minutes were not even cold yet, yet Dietershagen was already drinking to "peace"…

But there was something else that Obergefreiter Bergmann could not get over. Before he had destroyed the signal intelligence radio, there was one last radio report from the regimental headquarters in Falaise:

"Oberbefehlshaber (Commander-in-Chief) West recognizes Oberleutnant Dr. Dietershagen for the heroic resistance of his military base against the mighty foe with the Ritterkreuz (Order of the Knight's Cross)."

And there he stood now, Ritterkreuz recipient Dietershagen, still holding the Champagne bottle in his hand. "Oh my God, my dear God," murmured Hans Bergmann, and looked up to the sky spread peacefully over the ragged landscape, deep blue and healing…

The End

Notes on the Text: *Part 1: The Scylla of the Uniform*

Introduction

Apparently, the German Wehrmacht knew that some sort of invasion was being planned by the Allies, as Karlheinz notes several times throughout his text. However, not all German soldiers believed it was imminent. It is useful at this point to clarify the use of the term "invasion". This is what the Germans called June 6, 1944, what the French called "le Débarquement" (Disembarkation) and what we Americans called "D-Day". The term "invasion" depends, of course, on the beholder's eye. My father is *Feldwebel* (technical sergeant) "Erhard Gast" in the book.

Chapter 1

You will see the memoir changes in tone entirely after this pulpy beginning.

Chapter 2

My husband, Harry, and I had taken a trip to Normandy in 2018 to visit the various sites mentioned in the book and the American military cemetery in Colleville-sur-Mer. We actually were at this same radar station in Douvres-la-Délivrande, which is now the Radar Museum and open to visitors. Apparently the radar station resisted for 10 days following D-Day and after it finally surrendered to the British and Canadians, they found piles of German uniforms in a corner. It was a strange feeling to be in the same place my father had worked during the war. The real code name of the radar station was not "Goldfasan" (Golden Pheasant), but "Distelfink", the European equivalent of our goldfinch.

Chapter 3

This is the first instance where Erhard Gast (my father's character) stands up to his commanding officer, Dietershagen. Not only does he openly challenge him, he even somewhat mocks him. I can't believe Karlheinz really would have so openly challenged his superior in the German *Wehrmacht* during wartime. There was monitoring 24 hours a day at the Douvres-la-Délivrande radar station to keep track of enemy ships. That was my father's primary job, in somewhat of a supervisory capacity.

Chapter 4

Dietershagen was insisting on an old-fashioned form of military address to show deference, namely the 3rd person singular, "er" (he). Even though this form of address had largely fallen out of favor in the German military by World War II, Dietershagen probably insisted on it as a form of subtle humiliation.

I believe my father modeled the character of Ulrich Von Schütz on his best friend from childhood, Ulrich Von Otto. The "Von" designation is a signifier of former nobility, like "de" in French. After the war, Ulrich Von Otto took refuge with his aunt who lived in a castle at the Bodensee (Lake Constance) in Bavaria. He was also a German prisoner of war in the USA, at Fort Eustis in Newport News, Virginia. Ulrich was the last person my father took a trip to visit before he died of cancer in 1986.

Chapter 5

Gast and Von Schütz had both committed "unpardonable" offenses that kept them from becoming officers. This undoubtedly led to their close bond as like-minded friends. The exercise with the dog was yet another lesson in humiliation and subordination designed to keep the soldiers in line.

Chapter 6

Land on the southeastern coast of the Baltic Sea came under German rule in the Middle Ages. This area was called Preussen (Prussia) and had its own army run by the Prussian Junkers, who were the landed nobility of Prussia. After World War I, the Prussian Army ceased to exist and the German *Wehrmacht* replaced it, which during World War II developed from a purely German force into one in which significant numbers of foreigners from all over Europe served as volunteers. At the time of WWII, some Prussian principles still prevailed in the *Wehrmacht*, however: centralization, the primacy of the State, personal loyalty between commanding officers and their soldiers, and obedience. But also faults: narrow-mindedness, self-righteousness, a lack of imagination. This is what Karlheinz is referring to, including the tension between university-educated officers and those who worked their way up through the ranks.

Chapter 7

We know that the two friends are making their plans for the night of June 5th and, in retrospect, we also know what happened the next morning. The "D" in D-Day (June 6th, 1944) stands for "Day", so if June 6th was D, then June 5th was D - 1 and June 7th was D + 1. The walk that Von Schütz and Gast were planning to take was 3 kilometers, or about 2 miles, not too far on foot. Luc-sur-Mer (where the bunker was) is right on the coast, and Douvres-la-Délivrande (where the radar station was) is inland.

Chapter 8

Karlheinz is carefully chronicling the large and small humiliations that were part of German military life during World War II. He likes to point out casual cruelty or petty hypocrisy, which were probably legion.

Chapter 9

The *Atlantikwall* (Atlantic Wall) was an extensive system of coastal fortifications built by Nazi Germany between 1942 and 1944 during WWII as a defense against invasion from the United Kingdom. These fortifications comprised colossal coastal guns, batteries, mortars and artillery. They included "*Rommelspargel*" or "Rommel asparagus", 13- to 16-foot logs set at odd angles in the fields and meadows of Normandy. To discourage beach landings and to keep them from rotting in the water, they were sometimes inserted into steel pipes and were often invisible at high tide. They were named after *Generalfeldmarschall* (field marshal) Erwin Rommel.

Chapter 10

Karlheinz (aka Erhard) did indeed speak good French. He had a gift for languages and improved upon the French he had learned in school when stationed in France. He subsequently lived in France for almost 20 years. Curiously, he spoke grammatically correct, fluent French (although somewhat slowly) but never improved his comprehension of spoken French. This kept him from going to French movies or plays. His reading comprehension was excellent, however; after he had retired from the American company that sent him to France, he freelanced as a patent translator, even translating from French into English or German. He was not any kind of musician in real life, however.

Chapter 11

This is the first introduction of Hans Bergmann, the third member of the trio of "subversive" friends, who will play a prominent role in the second part of the novel. Karlheinz uses the introduction of this character to give a lot of compliments to Erhard Gast. My father was proud of the fact that despite his streak of subversiveness and his quiet disdain for his superiors, they continually sent to military training courses and promoted him. He never achieved the rank of full officer, however. He luckily also never saw actual combat because of this continuous military training. The three friends bonded tightly in their mutual contempt for their superiors, each by having flagrantly disregarded a direct order.

Chapter 12

On the night of June 5th, 1944, over 1000 British bombers dropped 5000 tons of bombs on German batteries in the Normandy assault area and 3000 Allied ships crossed the English Channel. They had postponed the invasion (named Operation Overlord) of occupied France repeatedly since May because of bad weather and tactical obstacles. General Eisenhower took advantage of the less than ideal weather; he may have thought that the Germans expected postponements because of the poor weather. June 5th was supposed to be D-Day, but they pushed it back by a day because the weather was even worse the day before.

Chapter 13

My father did not play the drums or any other instrument, but he was a fan of all kinds of music, especially classical and jazz. Neither did he sing, as far as I know, except for German carols on Christmas Eve. Here, as his alter ego Erhard Gast, he is an accomplished musician.

Chapter 14

Getting captured was obviously the better alternative for Dietershagen when getting killed was the other option. He was hoping to be captured by the Americans or the British because German soldiers had a fear of being captured by the Soviet troops, who had a reputation for brutality.

Chapter 15

Here we see the full extent of Dietershagen's cowardice and the contempt Karlheinz had for him. I wonder if he was a real person or a composite. This is one of the many, many questions I would have liked to ask my father.

Chapter 16

I know this is a fictional scene because the British, not the Americans, captured Karlheinz in the Sword Sector. The government of the United Kingdom requested American help with housing German prisoners of war because of a housing shortage in Britain, which is how my father ended up in Alabama after the British first sent him to Liverpool. Karlheinz was taken prisoner in his bunker at Luc-sur-Mer eight days after D-Day, on June 14th, when the soldiers in that bunker ran out of food and surrendered to the British. It may have served the consistency of the narrative better to leave out the British connection.

• • •

His capture is where *Part 1: The Szylla of the Uniform* ends and *Part 2: The Charybdis of the Barbed Wire* begins, which is the account of Karlheinz's imprisonment in the United States. He was transported on an American troopship from Liverpool to New York at the very end of June 1944, when he was about to turn 24, and from there to the German prisoner of war camp in Aliceville, Alabama.

Part 2: The Charybdis of the Barbed Wire

1. Camp Aliceville In Alabama, USA

For one hour already, the engines of the troop transport trucks crammed with German prisoners had been roaring along. The night was heavy. Bright stars looked down from the heavens. Wide and open lay the Alabama landscape and its highways, over which the trucks were now hurrying to their destination.

Erhard Gast, sitting with Ulrich Von Schütz and Hans Bergman, was right next to the tailgate, from which he could look out into the night. "Alabama, Mississippi, Florida," he was thinking to himself, "these are the southern states; this nearly forgotten part of the USA is called Dixieland. Oh, if only there were daylight, then one could at least see the details of the landscape!"

Suddenly, some lonely wooden houses appeared at the side of the road. The column of trucks slowed down; wide, leafy trees rushed by left and right and lights appeared everywhere: they were driving into a town. The houses were now closer together; a few Negroes walked by and looked curiously up at the live freight. Neon lights shone, jazz music rang out from bars lit up bright as day, and a movie palace with a snow-white facade appeared before the amazed eyes of the prisoners. Bright advertisements beamed from building walls: Armour—America's Luxury Home, General Electric Natural Color Tone Radios, Drink Coca-Cola, and others. Wide-eyed, Gast, Bergmann and Von Schütz stared at each other. This was America, the country in which they would live until the war finally ended.

■   ■   ■

Shortly after leaving the town, the transport trucks entered a big prisoner of war camp. It appeared to be a huge, spread-out, brightly lit village of barracks, surrounded by barbed-wire fences and watchtowers. A group of German administrative personnel already living there stood at the ready to show the new arrivals to their living quarters. Everything was quickly taken care of, and soon Gast, Von Schütz and Bergmann were sitting with their many comrades in the mess hall of the prisoner of war company, eating a serious welcome meal of hotdogs, fried potatoes, asparagus, cake, apricot compote and fresh, cold milk. Once they had sated their ravenous hunger with these delicacies, they climbed under the snow-white sheets of their side-by-side cots in the 50-person barracks to spend their first actual night under American skies. Before falling asleep, they assured each other over and over that they had imagined everything quite differently. Soon the room was quiet and the 50 men slept soundly, exhausted from their long trip into a new morning. And everything was so peaceful. There was no barrage of gunfire, and there were no fighter planes. Quiet, peace, sleep and dreams, relaxation, and even sheer bliss descended upon the men. This is how they slept their way into the first day in the camp, a day like many, many others to come.

2. Hans Bergmann Gets To Know His Wife

A few days later, Hans Bergmann stepped into the barracks in the morning, threw himself on his bed, and turned to Erhard Gast, who was just attaching the door to a nightstand he had built himself. "Do you know who just came to the camp on the new transport, Erhard?" he asked with a smile. "Our beloved Oberfeldwebel Kuklinski. I just spoke to him on the camp road. Oh, I'm telling you, he's not at all what he used to be. He was just creeping along, despondent and beaten-down. When I told him the three of us were all here, he said we should come visit him later. He's in Compound C, in Barracks 67—or was it 76? I don't know anymore."

"Of course," Gast said, "we'll go over right away. What do you think? How curious I am to see our dear old Stupi! He's going to have a hard time here, though! Nobody to boss around, no more roll call. That will sap all his energy, for sure."

As he said this, he hung the nightstand door on its hinges, placed the finished piece of furniture carefully next to his bed, lay back on his quilt and calmly regarded his loyal helper and former fellow shift worker at the analysis bunker. How nice that this was all behind them and that they were now what they had always wanted to be: just men, nothing but ordinary men.

Hans Bergmann, who had been lying on his back for some time, after a moment's reflection, pulled the rescued picture of his wife out of his luggage and regarded it tenderly, as he had so often done in the past few months. Oh yes, his Monika! What would he do if he didn't have her? Repeatedly, she had given him peace, strength, and happiness. Now he was a prisoner, and once again, a reunion with her was in the uncertain future. His thoughts wandered back to the days when he had gotten to know her in Heidelberg, shortly before the start of the war. His lodgings were in the garrison and he met her at the café Tosca, where she was working as a waitress in her father's restaurant. What

Bergmann experienced with her must have been more than a fleeting inclination, because they got married in 1942, after only two vacations spent together, the only vacations that Hans had had during the first two years of the war. One could barely describe the resulting marriage as a marriage. Only once more did Hans Bergmann have the good fortune to travel to Heidelberg to see his Monika and spend a few fleeting hours of happiness with her. Now, once there was no more travel ban, he would have been one of the first eligible to travel. But then came the Invasion and his capture as a prisoner of war.

Hans was still contemplating Monika's picture with an expression of intense longing as Erhard continued to read a book. For days, he had been urging Bergmann to speak often of his wife. Gast and Von Schütz had always listened with interest, and they shared his deep joy regarding the subject of his beloved wife. And even now, he felt compelled to talk about her again. The memories of her came rushing out of his mouth.

"You know, Erhard, during my last vacation, I tried to convince her not to serve in the café anymore. Old Man Barth agreed with my reasons. But they didn't have enough staff, and so it just wasn't possible to free her from having to work as a waitress."

Bergmann's voice was hoarse as Gast put his book away in order to give him his full attention. "It would have been a relief to me to not have her exposed anymore to the hungry looks of the many soldiers and students that are always hanging around the café Tosca. But,"—and here his voice cleared up—"she assured me I had nothing to worry about; she would never be unfaithful to me."

"Now let me see that picture for a change, Hans," said Gast. "I want to examine your Monika as thoroughly as you always do."

Laughing, Hans handed over his costly treasure, and watched, smiling, as Erhard Gast perused her features. Oh yes, you could clearly see from the picture that Hans's choice was not a bad one at all. Her face had fine and noble features, her eyes looked back at you open and full of adventure, her clothing and hairstyle choices were deliberate and tasteful. But his probing glance lingered on her lips for some time. Undoubtedly, she had a full and provocative mouth. It was entirely possible that this young woman had a strong streak of sensuality. Could that be?

"Hey Hans," asked Gast, "is your wife—how should I say this—of a willful and hot-blooded nature?"

"Well, what can I say?" responded Hans Bergmann thoughtfully, "usually she was rather cool and modest in her manner. Only once—I almost didn't recognize her—she literally burned with passion. That was when we said goodbye at the end of my last vacation. She kissed me like crazy and didn't want to let go of me. I had never seen her like that. Even on the train on the way back to my troop, I was a little shaken up, and—maybe this sounds strange—a little worried. But that feeling went away and then only happiness about her wild tenderness towards me remained."

Gast stared thoughtfully in front of him; Bergmann was silent. For a moment, there was not a sound. Then both of them got up to look for Kuklinski. Since Von Schütz had been helping as a translator in the communications barracks as of the early morning, the two went alone to Compound C.

Once they had passed hundreds of other prisoners on the main camp road and had turned into Compound C, they started looking for Barracks No. 67, which they soon found.

"I really don't know anymore if it was 67 or 76, but we'll try this one first," said Hans, opening the door. Like their own barracks, this one housed 50 men. As they strolled down the middle, they looked left and right at their newly arrived comrades lying on their cots, worn out from the trip. Kuklinski was not among them.

Just as Hans reached the door on the other side of the barracks, Gast discovered something that caused his heart to beat hard against his ribs. A young, red-haired sergeant was just pulling a picture out of his pack and standing it up on the wooden shelf next to his bed. It was—Erhard saw without a doubt—it was the same picture that Hans had just been looking at: the photograph of Monika Bergmann. But before Gast could regroup, Hans was already out the door. Erhard sprang after him, grabbed him by the arm, and quickly exclaimed: "I just saw something, Hans, that you should know about. I might be mistaken, but I really don't think I am." Uncomprehendingly, Hans stared back into his eyes. Erhard Gast continued, "In the barracks there's someone who has—of course it might mean nothing—but still: Someone just put the same picture of Monika that you have next to his bed."

Hans recoiled suddenly. "What are you saying?" he shouted in alarm. "A picture of Monika? The same one I have? Could it be her brother…? Can't be, he's dead. We have to go back right away…"

"Stop!" Erhard interjected urgently. "We have to think about this. To find out everything, you can't just barge in. We have to be smart about this. Pretend; remove all emotion from your voice and seem totally unconcerned. Most of all, say that you knew Miss Monika Barth only in passing, as a waitress in the café Tosca. Will you promise me to be sensible and in control of yourself? Keep in mind, a lot depends on your behavior in the next few minutes!"

"Alright," Hans answered hoarsely, "I'll try to act totally natural. Come on, let's go back." And as they turned around to return to the barracks they had just left, Hans Bergmann murmured quietly: "Dear God, be with me!"

When they had reached the sergeant's bed, both stopped and stared at the shelf next to it. Yes, there was Monika's picture, the same one that stood next to Hans Bergmann's bed over in Compound A. The sergeant to whom it belonged was lying on his bed in his boxer shorts, blinking lazily at the visitors with sleepy eyes. Hans walked slowly up to him and asked politely: "Um, excuse me; I would like to ask you something. The woman in the picture you have next to you, I know her slightly. Isn't she from Heidelberg?" After asking this question, he smiled tensely; a vein stood out sharply on his forehead.

The tired young man with the curly red hair and freckled face propped himself up on an elbow and answered in a desultory manner: "Yeah, that's right. Her name is Monika Bergmann, and she's a waitress at the café Tosca in Heidelberg. That's where I met her."

"And when was that, if I might ask?" Hans continued carefully, although he couldn't hide the slight tremor in his voice.

"Let's see, that was—," the red-haired young man said thoughtfully, "that was around the end of 1943. My posting was to a flak battery, right outside the city gates of Mannheim. I got to know her during the many quick trips I had to make to Heidelberg. Did you also once have something going on with her?"

Red splotches had appeared on Hans Bergmann's cheeks. With the same frosty smile as before, he answered carefully: "Yes, I already met her in 1939. I was also a soldier in Heidelberg. But—," he hesitated for a moment, "but, because she seemed a little loose in her morals, I gave up seeing her after we had gone to the movies together once or twice."

The freckled young man continued thoughtfully: "No—I think you might have been wrong about that. She was not at all easy. To get to my goal, I had to use all my seduction skills. I worked on her for weeks. I finally made it at Christmas and we spent the holidays together."

"Yes, but," interjected Hans in a quavering voice, "she must be married. Didn't you say her last name was Bergmann? I knew her as Monika Barth."

"Of course she was married. But you know how that is nowadays. She had only recently gotten married and her husband was on the battlefield; they didn't really know each other that well. At least that's what she told me once," he said with a grin.

Hans ran a trembling hand across his forehead, which had broken out in a light sweat. After a moment of agonized reflection, he pulled himself together and continued, "So if I understand correctly, you had a sort of meal ticket relationship with no strings attached? Is that right?"

"Yes, of course, that's what it was," the redhead replied nonchalantly. "But it became more than that, much more than that... behind her old man's back we were like two turtle doves, and we had some damn great times together—damn great, unforgettable times—if you really want to know; you can read what she wrote to me on the back of her picture. It speaks volumes. Here, look!"

With these words, he handed Hans the photo of Monika in its frame. Hans grabbed it quickly, turned it over, and read the following inscription together with Erhard Gast:

To you, my dearest boy, who consoled me in my loneliness, the comforting presence in my empty life
Forever yours, Moni

At this, Gast grabbed his friend firmly by the arm to keep him from doing something rash. But the latter only saw red. Seething, he tore his arm from Erhard's grasp, flung the picture to the floor with such force that shards of glass flew into the corners, balled his right hand into a fist, and was about to throw himself onto the redhead in a blind rage. As frightened men came running from all over the barracks, Gast pushed the raging man to the side and forced him to the door with short, hard blows. Gast wrenched the door open, pushed Hans roughly out, and held him in an iron grip as he implored him to calm down. After a few more feverish attempts to tear himself loose from Gast's grasp, Hans

Bergmann gave up. He shrank in upon himself and started sobbing in bewilderment; tears ran down his face.

The flustered redhead, who was suddenly at the door, cried out to Gast: "Oh my God, she's his wife!!" His realization seemed to hit him like a ton of bricks. He stood frozen on the threshold for a moment before disappearing back into the barracks, out of which curious onlookers continued to stream forth. All stood by silently. Only Hans Bergmann whimpered quietly, as Erhard Gast led him gently away.

3. The Story Of The Bald Pate

Some comrades in the barracks of our three friends discovered they had head lice. When they returned from the inspection area, they had bald heads. Peals of laughter broke out as the unlucky ones glumly examined their bald pates in the mirror. It was a remarkable sight. Their buddies were almost unrecognizable.

Von Schütz was especially gleeful at the spectacle of the bald ones. As he ran his sharp fingers over their shorn heads, he proudly assured them: "No sir, nothing like that will ever happen to me. If I had lice, I would prefer to stick my head under the faucet until all of them drowned; but a bald head—for me—out of the question!"

Following this loud proclamation he sauntered gracefully through the barracks hallway, running his hands through his overly long hair, which even here was especially cleanly and carefully cut. "Me and a bald head. No way! Ridiculous!" he repeated solemnly, "Not for a million bucks would I let them cut my hair off. You can offer me whatever you want! I would keep my hair no matter what." As peals of laughter resounded in response to this passionate declaration, he hurried to his bed to get in a little nap before lunch. At this, Gast laughingly said to him: "And what if you were to receive a firm offer, of very welcome and useful items, from well-meaning folks who would like nothing better than to see you—you of all people—shaved bald? Wouldn't you at least consider it? After all, we're behind barbed wire here, and in half a year it will all have grown back."

"Never, never," Ulrich replied, yawning but resolute. Then he slumbered peacefully.

By the time he awoke, Gast had prepared an offer, following lengthy negotiations with his barracks inmates. "Look at this list, my dear Ulrich, and you will see all the items you will get from us if you get your head shaved of your own free will: But study it carefully before you say no, because this kind of offer only comes around once in a lifetime." These were the words that Gast serenaded the newly awakened Ulrich Von Schütz with. Laughing, the latter grabbed the list, as a few curious men approached to gauge his reaction. Wow, all kinds of riches were being offered: pieces of clothing, furniture, beer, cigarettes, chocolate. "My God," he thought, "how nice it would be to have all of this. My $3 a month would almost all go towards the haircut." The temptation was just too great. "Yes," he said, plainly and calmly, "this is an offer I can accept." A loud, delighted cry filled the barracks. "But first hand it over, then you can cut."

Quick as a wink, they purchased the promised items at the canteen with the pooled money and placed them on his bed. He looked in wonderment at the colorful treasures. But he had little time for contemplation; the gathered mob thirsted after full contractual fulfillment. "Sit on the stool," yelled one of them, and, "Come on, Erhard, cut the mane off!" yelled another.

It didn't take long for it to be done. A man got up and went to the beer waiting at his bedside. Was that really Ulrich Von Schütz? That pitiful prisoner? That flat forehead, that egg-shaped head? Oh my God, what kind of transformation was this?

The cries of delight and peals of laughter just would not stop. Ulrich drank down two bottles of beer with the utmost dignity and restraint, then took up a mirror and glanced at it. His eyes glazed over. Apparently, he didn't even recognize himself. "This is what someone looks like who has just seen a ghost..." he thought to himself.

.   .   .

A few days later, upon the occasion of a recreational evening program organized by the Company, Ulrich Von Schütz, with his stubbly head, stepped up to the podium and recited a self-penned epic. In one fell swoop, he became the most popular man in his entire section of the camp. Here it is:

"The Story Of The Bald Pate."

4. Now I Know What We Are Fighting For!

Roughly two months had gone by and brought all kinds of changes. Since Hans Bergmann had had to face the true nature of his wife, not much could be done with him anymore, and Erhard Gast's remorse over bringing to light the discovery of the picture in the young sergeant's quarters came too late. Hans had completely lost himself in bitterness and despair. A deep disconnect with the world around him had transformed him into a hard-to-stomach, brooding loner. Luckily, Ulrich Von Schütz could intervene, since he was now the head company interpreter, by having him assigned as an orderly in the camp military infirmary. So at least he could stay at Camp Aliceville, while all the other men in the enlisted ranks transferred to work camps.

The enormous Camp Aliceville was now filled with roughly 6000 captured NCOs and sergeants. According to the Geneva Convention, these ranks did not have to work. Therefore, except for a handful of typists, interpreters, artisans and orderlies, thousands just hung around: They played soccer, took walks inside the camp, saw movies and plays, studied or taught (Gast led an English class) at a well-equipped camp school, and started passionately discussing and arguing amongst themselves.

A dangerous controversy started spreading throughout the camp. It became more inflamed and helped to spread increasing discord, hate, animosity and risk. This is how it came about. Roughly 4000 of the prisoners came from the new invasion front in the Normandy region of France. They had experienced something that the remaining 2000 prisoners, captured in Africa over a year earlier, could not even imagine: the indisputable superiority of the Allied powers. Many of the "Normandists" expressed their views accordingly. They often spoke out against the Nazis, arguing that the further conduct of warfare was pointless, and summarily dismissing the illusion of any notion of conquest.

The "Africans" felt entirely differently. The majority were jingoistic, militaristic, and extreme Nazis. Slowly but surely, they took control of the key positions in the camp. By the fall of 1944, they had definitively gotten the upper hand and had set up a small Nazi state within Camp Aliceville, governed by terror and threats.

Soon it came about that one could no longer speak out at all against the Nazis or the insanity of the war without risking a beating. Hundreds of "Normandists" converted to the "African" way of thinking, and only a tiny number of sworn anti-Fascists remained. They had to stay under the radar and keep their mouths shut. Life in Camp Aliceville became dangerous for them. Every few days, Nazi spies hunted down one or more of them and beat them with truncheons until they were half dead. The American camp administration, which was kept informed by their German counterparts in the camp, did everything in their power to protect the anti-Fascists. But they could not succeed. The reign of terror was too powerful.

This gave rise to the "defector movement". Men who had said too much, and wanted to be spared the Nazis' wooden or iron clubs, gave themselves up to American protection, leaving the camp under this protection. This was, however, a very dangerous undertaking. Nazi thugs intercepted shortly beforehand, one man who tried during daylight hours to slip out of the camp gate with his duffel on his back. As he was suffering from a double skull fracture and several bleeding wounds, American guards carried him to the camp infirmary. German doctors who worked there, in conspiracy with the Nazi leaders, were loath to treat this "Communist"; American doctors had to treat the badly wounded prisoner in their own hospital.

Following this incident, the defectors proceeded more cautiously. They secretly tipped off the American soldiers who worked side by side with German administrators in the orderly room of the prisoner of war camp, then left the camp as if they were innocently taking a walk. A few minutes later, their packed bags would be driven out of the camp in an American Jeep.

Gast and Von Schütz, who had not been at all shy about expressing their disgust with war, militarism and the Nazi terror, had gone quiet. Grinding their teeth, they had outwardly resigned themselves to the situation. But inwardly they burned with a seething frustration. They simply could not comprehend the unfathomable phenomenon that their fellow citizens would suppress the freedom of thought and expression that existed even here behind barbed wire, with such brutal enforcement tactics. This was the German boot personified.

Ulrich Von Schütz suffered the most under the terrible conditions in the camp. Once when he was in the mess hall buying the American-inspired prisoner of war newspaper "Der Ruf" (The Call), boycotted by the Nazi camp leaders but offered for sale to the German prisoners on orders from the Americans, one of the Nazis ripped it from his hands. Ulrich seethed with rage and racked his brain with what they could do to contain these overpowering oppressors.

To the Nazi oppressors, Ulrich had long been a thorn in the company's side. There was no shortage of attempts to oust him from his interpreter post. But because he was good friends with the American soldier Private Louis Wolfe, known as Lou, an administrative superior in the company, all such efforts came to naught. This made the Nazis' blood boil. He was probably the most disliked man in the company. As he strode up front next to Lou at the daily prisoner count, insults and threats were constantly being called out to him.

Because he was well aware of the constant danger that surrounded him, he had an iron bar at the ready behind his bed, just like Gast and Bergmann. In case of an attack by terrorists, the three friends were ready to band together and defend each other to the end. Neither of the other two wanted to defect because the greatest danger of all was to Ulrich, and he had no desire to leave his key position.

. . .

Then it happened at noon one day, as most of the prisoners were lying sleepily on their beds, digesting the excellent food that was always being served. Ulrich had returned to the orderly room, while Erhard and Hans dozed on their quilts. Suddenly, a loud cry from outside shattered the noontime stillness. Gast and Bergmann startled up from their beds. That sounded like... Wasn't that...? The cry rang out again. Gruesome. Full of mortal fear. "Hey Hans, that's Ulrich!" Gast shouted in horror. Nearly everyone had jumped off their beds and was running outside. Gast and Bergmann also ran out of the barracks. Outside, they could just make out the tail end of a mob of men armed with clubs as they disappeared behind the barracks where the orderly room was; they were throwing their weapons away and crawling quick as a flash through holes in the fence that led to the neighboring camp compound, so that they could duck behind some barracks there.

Meanwhile, the men roused by the cries ran as fast as they could behind the orderly room barracks. What they saw there was unspeakable, and for a few seconds there was dead silence. Ulrich Von Schütz lay wheezing on the ground. They had beaten his upturned face to a bloody pulp. He lay motionless in his torn and bloodstained clothes.

Private Louis Wolfe was standing next to him, with a facial expression no one had ever seen before. His eyes, shifting back and forth between the badly beaten man and the watching Germans, sparked with rage. There was still no sound. Then came the words, raw and hoarse, forced from between the lips of the American: "God damn—now I know what we are fighting for!" Then he bent down, lifted Ulrich gently from the ground, laid him over his shoulder, and carried him out of the camp, as his uniform slowly turned dark red from Ulrich's blood.

As he left, the crowd roiled. The beast came out in them. "That ass sure got what he deserved!" "He won't dare open his trap again!" "That's what should happen to all those enemies of the state!" "I hope the jerk is finally dead!" Their voices swirled together.

The crowd was moving and was closely following behind Lou, who was carrying Ulrich toward the camp exit, eyes fixed straight ahead. A faint trickle of blood followed in his wake. The mob continued to heckle the beaten man with increasing volume. How great was their desire to grab the lifeless one and stamp on him on the ground! But Lou had already arrived at the camp exit. At the last moment, something terrible occurred. Thrown by someone in the mob, a clunky wooden shoe came flying towards Ulrich as he was hanging over Lou's shoulder. It hit him in the head and opened up a fresh wound, which bled freely, blood seeping in between the stubbly hairs. The Nazis howled with glee. But Bergmann and Gast were heartbroken. They were beside themselves with raging fury and utter despair.

5. The Kangaroo Court

Only Hans Bergmann's work kept him going. The doctors and orderlies of the German camp infirmary, who were operating under strict orders from the Americans to treat fully all victims of politics, were working flat out. Bergmann usually returned only late at night to the barracks, informing his grimly listening bed neighbor Erhard shortly before they fell asleep of the condition of the newly arrived beating victims. He tended to the gravely wounded Ulrich with tender loving care. His wounds were slowly healing, and according to Bergmann, the attack would probably leave his face with no outer deformity except for a few scars.

Erhard Gast had been in close contact with the camp's anti-fascist underground movement for a few days now. The situation did not at all appear hopeless. The secret group was in a suitable position to effect counter-espionage. Its members sat unrecognized amid the Nazi camp leadership, among the editors of the camp newspaper, in the library, in the school, camouflaged among the orderlies and clerks who served as liaisons to the American camp office, and especially in the religious worship communities of both the Lutherans and the Catholics. Now and then subcommittees of the underground resistance gathered to discuss defense counter-tactics. Sometimes they met in the camp church's vestry, other times in a library storage room, or even in the dressing rooms of a theater barracks.

It was all very dangerous, as the Nazis did everything possible to expose the members of the secret fifth column who were undermining their efforts from within. In order to imbue their regime of beatings with some sort of "regulatory" legitimacy, they even engaged in establishing a kangaroo court of sorts.

No matter how secretly they conducted this undertaking, it was impossible to keep the underground movement in the dark about this new abomination. Without fail, Nazi plans found their way into the hands of the resistance, who carefully studied them in the camp church's vestry.

SS-Oberscharführer (SS-Senior squad leader) Finkler was supposedly in charge of the kangaroo court. The anti-Fascists knew him well, since as company leader of Compound C, he had distinguished himself as an especially zealous instigator regarding the persecution of the so-called "Defeatists". Among the court participants was Kuklinski, as Gast discovered while studying the plans with Pastor D. Galler. "So then, Kuklinski is in the kangaroo court; that's a fine kettle of fish," Erhard thought grimly to himself.

Gast's frequent absences, his distancing himself from the company, his friendship with the "criminal" Von Schütz and the equally suspect Bergmann, all earned him a preferred spot atop the Nazis' blacklist. Because they thought of him as very intelligent and because he spoke excellent English, they assumed he was a leader of the anti-Fascist underground movement. But they couldn't prove it.

As several members of the "Reds" (as the Nazis succinctly named the anti-Fascists) gathered once more at a secret meeting in the vestry, one of their most reliable liaisons to the Nazi camp command ran in excitedly, reporting on the very first session of the kangaroo court, which had taken place the previous evening. Nothing from this session had trickled out so far, so this report caused a veritable sensation. Fortunately, this information gave the anti-Fascists some precious pointers.

The court met in the "Temple", a barracks room in which the Nazis ran "education courses", during which they mocked the Americans and indefatigably touted the upcoming German victory.

During the first meeting of the court, which had lasted from midnight until about 4:00 in the morning, reported the agent, Pastor D. Galler had received a death sentence as punishment for his conspiracy against the State. The sentence was supposed to be carried out on the ultimate day of German victory. There were no other details available.

For the next court session, on February 12, 1945, the following were to be tried: Feldwebel Gast, Fähnrich Siedler, Unteroffizier Burdach and Unteroffizier Bär. The Nazis were obviously very much in the know, since the four named were all key members of the anti-Fascist movement.

"We must learn more about this," stated Pastor Galler. "But how?" "I would like to take on this assignment," said Erhard Gast, "since it affects me personally. Not to worry, we will definitely find out more about the next session of this kangaroo court." After the meeting, the participants left the church barracks at different times, using different exits.

.   .   .

SS-Oberscharführer Finkler stood up and intently regarded the men before him. Ten men, all dressed in their German military uniforms, seated at a long table illuminated by wax candles, looked gravely back at him. Blankets covered the windows so that no light was visible from the outside. A homemade German Reich battle flag adorned with a huge swastika hung on the front of the rectangular podium next to the table.

Finkler, whose collar had white SS runes cut from paper pasted to it, spoke. He surely was not thinking at this moment of how he had torn the now so boastfully replaced runes from his uniform in abject fear at the moment he became a prisoner, but only of the "Federal traitors" he now had to sentence with the help of his accomplices. His words, however, were not only being heard by the men seated at the table but also by another, crouching behind the flag in the wooden box of the podium, one who had a pretty good view of the general proceedings through a small hole in the flag's fabric. This crouching, listening observer was Erhard Gast.

"Given that the long arm of our respectable German law cannot reach the traitors, the enemies of the State, and the defeatists in our own ranks," began Finkler in a near-whisper, "we are meeting here in order to sentence those who wish to sabotage our lawful undertakings to their rightfully earned punishment."

As he paused theatrically, and as some participants nodded in agreement, Erhard Gast stretched his muscles in the narrow confines of the podium as much as was possible so that he didn't get cramps. SS-Oberscharführer Finkler continued, somewhat louder: "Our Führer expects us to intercede for him under every circumstance, and so it is our solemn duty to establish administrative and penal structure where there is none in his stead. For this reason, we are performing a very special favor for our beloved Führer with the establishment of this court, for which he will surely repay us many fold at the victorious end of the war."

"With this, I come to the reason we are all here. Today we are charging the traitors, whom we now want to sentence one by one. First, Feldwebel Erhard Gast. He is undeniably guilty of playing a leading role in the traitorous underground movement here in the camp. In addition, he makes up and spreads defeatist news, praises the Americans' pseudo-culture, criticizes the German government, slanders the blessed defensive war waged by the German people as if it were something unjust, stands in close conspiracy with the Church (sworn enemy of the State), and uses his English language classes to spread propaganda about the supposed superiority of the Anglo-Saxon/American race over the German one. In consequence of all these offenses, I move that Feldwebel Gast should receive the death penalty."

"Unteroffizier Karsten, you are in the same company as the accused, and you are a student in his English class as well. Please, tell us, do you feel that the accusation as just presented is justified?"

Curious, Erhard placed his eye as close as possible to the hole in the flag as his English student, Karsten, stood up. That crook! How he had always irritated him with his fake-chummy questions. That's why! One just couldn't be careful enough in here. These good-for-nothings were everywhere.

"Yes, well," Karsten began confidently, "Feldwebel Gast is, without a doubt, one of the most dangerous ones. He hates our Führer and the Nazi movement like the plague. One can tell by his manner, the things he says, and especially by the company he keeps. He regularly visits that Communist traitor Von Schütz in the camp hospital, he openly praises the American films that he's constantly watching, and in the English class he teaches, he recently claimed that the English language has a lot more words than German, which makes it especially useful and rich. Then he regularly attends church services, and recently said that all wars are madness. In addition, he regularly reads the American scandal sheets 'Time', 'Life', and 'The New York Times'. I have often observed how happy he is when reading these publications. He probably takes great joy in the false reports of our supposed retreat. In short, Feldwebel Gast is, just like his friend the Pastor, a dangerous enemy of the State, whom we have to eradicate from our society of upstanding Germans!" These were Karsten's last words, and he sat down contentedly. Finkler, who had taken a quick look at his meeting protocol, responded: "Many thanks, Karsten. Your indications suffice fully to sentence the accused, but we still want to hear from Gast's former company comrade, Oberfeldwebel Kuklinski. What can you add to the case against Gast?"

"Oh, that's very simple," the latter answered quickly. "Feldwebel Gast is an especially rotten apple. He is one of those know-it-all intellectuals. In the company, he was so underhanded as to keep all the important, prestigious assignments for himself. Even though he was the opposite of what you would expect from a soldier, he still made himself indispensable. He had his fingers in everything. Because of his constant need to elevate himself, he even made use of his officer status to alter completely the monthly reports I wrote in the orderly room, passing them on to the Regiment in an entirely novel form. He was exercising sabotage even then. If he was ever in charge of the drill or field training, everything was completely relaxed. Not an ounce of discipline! Once, I saw him lying in a trench with some of the enlisted men on the Blue Team telling each other jokes, while the Red Team was launching a surprise attack on the line. As they charged the trench, I heard him yell: 'Enough of war, time for dinner; that's much more important, anyway!' So he was always trying to undermine our fighting spirit. Once, he had to give a speech about the upcoming invasion. He was clear that he thought the German coastal defense was incapable of holding back the enemy invasion. The boss wanted to imprison him for that. It was only because the invasion took place that he didn't end up in prison."

"Based on everything I know about Feldwebel Gast, I have to agree with Karsten: this man is unfit to serve the German Reich. He will always remain an enemy of the State and we must therefore eliminate him."

Following Kuklinski's comments, it didn't take even five minutes for the kangaroo court to condemn Erhard Gast to death. This was also the case for the other three accused men. But the participants couldn't agree on the best method to achieve their ends.

"We should string up the condemned on the camp fence at night, using nooses prepared in advance," said one. Since Finkler met this suggestion with a shake of his head, another spoke up: "I suggest we scatter finely cut hair into their food. They'll get acute appendicitis, which will lead to a quick death." "That's not guaranteed!" Finkler interjected, "and anyway, we would have to make their corpses disappear."

"I have the solution," said a participant. "We finish the traitors off at night in their beds with iron bars. Then we drag the corpses into the showers and chop them up into little pieces so that we can burn them right away in the heating system's coal fire." "Excellent!" cried Finkler. "Let's stick with this plan; then we can get rid of the evidence all at once."

The death sentences were to be carried out with the undoubtedly soon-to-come celebration of assured victory.

6. The Most Beautiful Woman In The World

The time until the ultimate surrender passed like a bad dream. The massacre that the Nazis planned had never come to pass, because immediately after the first session of the kangaroo court, the American camp administration took swift action. Through weeks of hard work, the underground movement had established a comprehensive list on which they left out not a single rabble-rouser, club-beater, terrorist, chauvinist or militarist. In a well-organized and lightning-quick operation, the Americans transferred these black sheep to another camp shortly before the ultimate surrender took place.

Thereafter, the nightmarish conditions that had weighed so heavily on the camp gradually faded away. There were no more beatings, and one could speak freely again.

Following the capitulation of Germany, the higher military ranks started working as well. They could refuse, but this happened rarely. Food rations for non-workers were so meagerly apportioned that one did much better as a worker. This led to the dissolution of the larger Non-Commissioned Officer camps. Even Camp Aliceville was affected, and they transferred the prisoners to various work camps in small groups.

Most of the prisoners remained in the area around Aliceville. Erhard Gast was also affected. Because the camp infirmary remained in place, Erhard was separated from Hans Bergmann, who was not one of those transferred. Erhard Gast also said goodbye with a heavy heart to Ulrich Von Schütz, who was slowly getting better.

Erhard came to the tiny new work camp, located directly on the outskirts of Aliceville, with mixed feelings. He missed the library, the camp school, the theaters and his treasured free time. It was now the month of June, and the hot Alabama sun shone relentlessly down from the sky. The first work assignment on the farms in the area was to stack peanut plants to dry around a vertical wooden stake in the ground. The farmers expected every worker to produce 24 stacks per day. This was backbreaking work, and it was no surprise that everyone disappeared into bed shortly after returning to the camp every evening.

Erhard Gast functioned as the workgroup's leader and interpreter. This assignment did not, however, excuse him from his stacking requirements, but caused him a great deal of additional work, especially regarding language interpreting and representing the interests of the prisoners. Because he showed a true aptitude for getting along with Mr. White, the farmer in charge of his group, he was very well-liked by his 12 fellow workers.

Every once in a while, Mr. White would want more than the usual amount stacked. If the work was progressing nicely for the men, if he had provided a decent lunch at noon, and if the sun was not burning all too hot, the group was open to further negotiation and happily stacked longer in return for the appropriate monetary compensation. Once they had accomplished the work, their pay would be drunk in liquid form at an American beer bar before Mr. White drove the men back to the camp in his open-bed farm truck.

Once, in the course of such an evening drinking party, Mr. White made a joyful offer: "Boys, tonight I will show you the most beautiful woman in the world. I'm telling you, you have seen nothing like her."

"Yeah, well, who's that, Mr. White?" Erhard asked, somewhat curiously. "My wife, of course!" answered the farmer, as he dusted cigar ash off the front of his greasy overalls. "She'll amaze you, boys; you have never seen such beauty and grace. We'll drive by my house, I'll call my wife to come to the door, you can take a quick look at her from the truck, and then we'll drive right back to camp. Would you like that?"

"Sure, we'd like that," answered Erhard, after he had quickly translated Mr. White's surprising offer to the Germans.

As Mr. White's truck with the 13 prisoners of war standing in its open bed behind the side walls pulled up to his wooden house in Aliceville, 26 pairs of eyes trained themselves expectantly on the front door, which stood just behind a small lawn, in the shadow of several walnut trees.

"Mammy, come on out, will you?" Mr. White called out in an authoritative voice, as the curiosity of the prisoners, evermore eager to see the most beautiful woman in the world, steadily mounted.

The door of the colorful wooden house slowly opened, and a woman stepped out into the open. Was this the beauty for whom the wagon had stopped? Oh yes, it was indeed her, and she was returning the smiles of the 13 men somewhat embarrassedly. If the prisoners had expected a movie goddess because of Mr. White's proud promises they were now disappointed, as Mrs. White was short and plump, wore a colorful work apron, had her white hair coiffed in an old-fashioned style, balanced a huge pair of glasses on her nose, and laughed at them through a mouth dominated by a snow-white pair of dentures, framed by a chubby double-chin and two round, apple-red cheeks. Yet—and all would acknowledge this—she was indeed the most beautiful woman in the entire world.

The amazed men continued to stare at the sweet old lady as she stared back at them.

"Let's go, boys," called out Mr. White, as he started up the truck without having given his wife a word of explanation. The truck rolled slowly forward as the prisoners waved to Mrs. White until she disappeared from view behind the walnut trees.

7. Pitt Kisses Molly

Once the peanut harvest was over, there was a new transfer. The small harvest camp was supposed to remain empty until next summer, and they transferred all its inhabitants to the giant army hospital in Tuscaloosa, Alabama. This hospital was like a small town filled to the rafters with wounded American soldiers.

Newly arrived prisoners mostly worked as handymen, cleaners and kitchen personnel. But they also had to cut grass, work on road crews and chop wood. Erhard Gast's work assignment was as an interpreter in the company's orderly room, which pleased him to no end. This way he could further his language skills and had an hour or two of free time here and there, which was not the case for the others.

In the evenings, when the day's work was done, he liked to stroll through the small camp. Usually he walked alone, sunk in thought, filled with the images of his memory.

Once, when he was wandering along the barbed wire fence, he came upon a young fellow prisoner sitting on a rock, with a notebook on his pulled-up knees in which he was writing something.

As he passed, their eyes made contact and the young prisoner suddenly asked Erhard: "Can you please tell me what something is in English?"

"Of course," Erhard replied in a friendly manner. "What would you like to know?"

"Oh, just something minor," the questioner said hastily, "how do you say, 'ich möchte dich gerne küssen' (I would like to kiss you)?"

Erhard Gast stared at him in amazement. Smiling curiously, he looked into the blue eyes of the young man sitting across from him. "Why, in God's name, do you want to know that?"

"Well, here's the thing," the young man answered, trying hard to appear nonchalant. "The world is full of adventure, always and everywhere, even here. You only have to grab hold of the opportunity and the good fortune that presents itself. Even as a prisoner of war, you can have an adventure. Of course, not in as grand a style as in the past. But if you have the courage and the conviction and a dash of romanticism in your blood, then life has something special waiting for you, even as a prisoner of war. You just have to grab hold at the right moment."

Now silent, as if relieved after making this extensive declaration, he looked expectantly towards Erhard.

After a moment of reflection, the latter replied: "In theory, I totally agree with you. But despite my sympathy with your romantic impulses, I can't possibly imagine where you would find the opportunity in a place like this to be alone with a beautiful woman, and be able to tell her 'I would like to kiss you'!"

"Ha, ha!" the blue-eyed young man laughed triumphantly, "that's not at all impossible for me. I work alone on the grounds of the hospital, unsupervised except for an old American plumber who is like a father to me. How often he even lets me repair heating ducts or water pipes all by myself! And so you see how I'll be able to make the acquaintance of a young lady during such an opportunity."

And so he asked again, with even more urgency than before: "So how do you say 'ich möchte dich gerne küssen'?"

"I would like to kiss you," replied Erhard.

"Wait, wait, not so fast!" he interjected hastily. "Say it again, so I can write it down phonetically."

As requested, Erhard repeated himself, as he smilingly watched the eagerly writing young kiss-seeker. The sun, which was just setting below the horizon, threw the shadows of the watchtower and some rows of barbed wire onto the young man hunched over his notebook.

When he had finished, Erhard Gast asked him: "Hey, what's your name, anyway?"

Concentrating on Erhard once more, he quickly answered: "It's Pitt, but recently I've been calling myself Pitty, with a 'y' at the end, because it sounds more American." And with a laugh, he added: "You have to have the ability to fit in anywhere. That's the secret!"

. . .

After this encounter, the two saw each other every evening. Usually Pitty brought his big notebook on their walks around the camp, in order to add to his number of English sentences for everyday use. Illustrative of the general direction of his imagination, these were all the same type: "I'm so happy when you are around me. I see you in all my dreams. My love for you has no end. I will love you forever." This was the general tenor of his useful sentences, which he diligently learned by heart after writing them down in his own phonetic script. He knew nothing about grammar and such, but his proficiency was adequate enough, in his own opinion, to seduce a beautiful American woman, which was his primary goal.

Several evenings went by in conversation, phonetic writing sessions, and talk of Pitt's romantic hopes for the future, until, yes, until he came running towards Erhard, who had just returned to the camp after work, at breakneck speed, and threw his arms enthusiastically around him, joyfully blurting out: "I did it, I kissed her: Imagine, I kissed Molly on the mouth! Oh—I have to tell you all about it, right away, now, at once!" Then he swallowed hard a few times, slowly got himself under control, and began, "So, it was like this":

"Mr. McCormick, my sixty-year-old boss, was making the rounds with me through the hospital, as usual. His work orders today were for the usual locations: the toilets in the WAC quarters weren't flushing, one of the washing machines in Main

Kitchen D wasn't draining, they couldn't turn off the water faucet in Ward 18."

"First, we went to Kitchen D because it was the closest to us."

"As usual, amputated American soldiers wearing maroon bathrobes were being pushed around in wheelchairs by pretty nurses. Luckier men with more minor wounds were strolling along the garden paths with their heavily made-up sweethearts, and all around us nurses, WACs, White and Black civilians, hurried to their work locations. Only a few even noticed the big, black PW on my clothes. Most of them didn't give me or Mr. McCormick a second look as we walked through the big hospital grounds with our tool bags."

"When we arrived at Kitchen D, one of the huge Negro cooks told us what needed to be repaired on the washing machine drain. I saw right away where the problem was, and unpacked my tools to fix it myself, without Mr. McCormick's help."

"Smiling to himself, my old boss watched my preparations, suddenly realizing that he would now have time to breakfast in one of the many canteens while I did all the work. So I watched my good old master plumber boss happily shuffle out of the kitchen entryway, where he had left me all by myself with my wrench and the washing machine."

"A glass door separated the room in which I found myself from the kitchen, through which I could see the White and Black cooks and dishwashers walking around. White steam rose from enormous pots every time someone lifted the lid, and the smell of freshly baked cake made its way even over to me."

"Just as I was unscrewing the drain of the washing machine, the door to the kitchen opened and a feminine being came out with short, mincing steps. This personage stood out to me because she was a different feminine being than the ones I was normally familiar with, namely because she was Black: Black as the night, or like oven soot, or like dark chocolate."

"The young lady had full, but not too full, lips and uncommonly attractive eyes. As she glanced to the side, the whites of her eyes flashed like puffs of whipped cream in dark brown hot chocolate."

"The young Negro lady tapped closer in her elegant shoes perched on high heels. Her simple white-and-red-checked work dress with its dainty white apron stood out in contrast to her fashionable footwear."

"As she passed the washing machine, which I was kneeling in front of, I greeted her. I want to say it was reflexively, because I hadn't planned on it or considered it beforehand. I made my salutation as I looked deep into her jungle eyes and smiled as I lifted my wrench in greeting. Oh, how her indifferent expression changed! She saw herself being greeted, not only by a White man, but by one who was kneeling before her. That did not seem to be her everyday experience, as evidenced by her startled reaction to my attentiveness. Confused, she thanked me for my greeting by parting her full lips in a charming smile, uncovering two rows of big, ivory-white teeth, and with all the feminine grandeur she could muster she lifted the pointer finger of her right hand coquettishly to the level of her eyes in a return salutation, followed by running quickly and somewhat embarrassedly out of the room to the other side."

" 'She is a young, pretty, strapping woman,' I realized. And suddenly I had a great idea: What if I were to try out some of my memorized sentences on her, including my offer of a kiss? My God! The idea hit me like a ton of bricks. That was definitely a possibility! I was alone in here. And the entire situation hit me as so exotic, so romantic, that the prospect of succeeding made me feel quite dizzy."

"While I was alone and waiting for her return, I quickly went through my repertoire: 'I'm so happy when you are around me. I see you in all my dreams'—and—my blood raced faster: 'I would like to kiss you! I... would... like'..."

"The door opened behind me. She had come back. I spun around and stared yearningly into her eyes. I followed her from my kneeling position with eager eyes until she reached me. Then—what was happening? — she halted suddenly, looked down at me for half a second, and asked shyly: 'Are you hungry'?"

"Wait a minute, hungry means 'hungrig,' I suddenly realized. During the few moments I was reflecting on this, she was already pointing to her mouth and making chewing motions. 'How cute!' I thought and hurried to stand up and say 'Yes, yes,' accompanied by vigorous nodding."

"She happily sprang back to the kitchen and returned with a glass of milk and three giant pieces of freshly baked apple cake."

"Somewhat awkwardly, but happy to have been of service to the White man who had greeted her, she handed the much-appreciated gift to me, as a smooth, black strand of hair escaped her pretty bun, which made her sweet bewilderment even more attractive."

"Not knowing what to do now, she continued to stand uncertainly in front of me. 'OK, buddy, now's the time to act!' was the thought that shot through my mind, 'now or never!' And I was already hearing myself asking, totally natural: 'Please, tell me, what's your name?' Oh, how her face brightened! Somewhat fearfully, she looked around to make sure we really were all alone, then said: 'Molly,' her full lips coming to a point at the 'M' in her name. 'And your name?' she asked me boldly, her head tilted expectantly. Her dark face had reddened slightly."

"'Pitty,' I answered cheerily. Looking at me, she tenderly murmured 'Pitty!' and I in the same tone of voice, 'Molly'!"

"Now nothing can go wrong anymore, I realized with a start! Act now, quickly and decisively, that's the ticket!"

"As I carefully took a half step behind the washing machine, I spoke, smiling, to the dark face, now fully turned towards me: 'Molly, I would like to kiss you!' My hands reached for her shoulders and I tenderly whispered once more: 'Molly, Molly, I would like to kiss you'!"

"'Really?' she whispered, barely audible, flooded with surprise and happiness. She closed her eyes in rapture, thrust out her full lips, and presented them to me, trembling, to be kissed. And I dove into her mouth, into this so willingly offered affection, and sucked out an endless string of kisses until both she and I were totally out of breath. Only then did we stop..."

"As I paused, she took a step back, drew a deep and trembling breath into her lungs, pressed her hand onto her heart, and a gurgling, jungle cry of joy escaped her half-open, hotly kissed mouth. Then, with a start, she turned around and hurried away with her tapping gait and heaving chest, in the swelling splendor of her Black limbs."

8. A Man Goes Into The Hut

As two years of captivity had run their course, the circle closed for Erhard Gast: he came back to Camp Aliceville, which they had converted to a repatriation camp in the meantime. Within several-week intervals, prisoners outfitted for home left the camp in groups of 6000 at a time to make way for new columns of troops. Nobody knew for sure if they were really going to Germany. The American side did not expound on the destination of the voyage in response to questions, so a rumor firmly took hold that they were being transferred to Great Britain or France. The uncertainty led to anxiety, worry, and, mostly, fear.

To his immense joy, Erhard ran into his friend Hans Bergmann at the hospital. He had spent all the past two years in the hospital as an orderly, and they had not yet targeted him for repatriation. As he sorrowfully told Erhard, they would not release the hospital orderlies until the very end. And that could take several more months.

It startled Erhard when he saw Hans again, as he made a scattered, nervous impression and had a strange look in his eye. What could that mean? Erhard was full of concern for his good old friend. Had his soul actually been harmed during the long months of incarceration? Hans Bergmann's first news was that Ulrich Von Schütz had been back in the camp for about 14 days now. After his recovery a year ago, they had sent him to a work camp, but now he was back and slated for repatriation.

As soon as Erhard had gotten the camp section and barracks number of his other friend, he hurried out of the hospital to go find Ulrich. He was very excited: On the same day, he would finally get to see both of his beloved buddies again. What joy! How could Ulrich be doing? Would he still be wearing his self-tailored white bush shirt? And what would his hair look like? Would he have his old artist's mane back?

Full of anticipation, Erhard hurried along the main camp road in the light of the arc lamps shining through the evening darkness. Compound D, Barracks 47. When he arrived at Ulrich's quarters, several of his comrades told him that Ulrich had left some time ago, probably bound for the canteen to play Skat (a German card game). Erhard turned on his heel and stepped back out into the velvety darkness, from which comforting lamplight shone everywhere. Taking a deep breath of the warm summer air, he stood still for a moment, and rested deep in thought before making his way to the canteen. He thought of his upcoming reunion with Ulrich, full of joyful anticipation. He saw him in his imagination, smiling gleefully, with his crooked beard and his dancer's walk.

"Oh, Ulrich, you dear fellow sufferer," he murmured. He was still standing next to the barracks when an easy, lighthearted feeling overtook him. He was suddenly a little dizzy and the dark night air pressed up softly against his head and limbs. Dreamily, he looked up. There—over there—came Ulrich! As if floating on air, he appeared out of the darkness and stepped into the light circle of a streetlamp. His bush shirt was glowing stark white as, without a sound, he took some small, jerky steps, like a marionette, up the wooden steps of the barracks about 20 meters away from Erhard. He looked so strange, almost ghostly! Now Ulrich's head was directly under the light bulb at the entrance to the hut and his blonde hair shimmered like a halo.

As Erhard tried to call out to Ulrich, his voice failed. Startled, he tried again, and this time he could speak. His voice sounded overly shrill, loud, and foreign to him: "Ulrich, Ulrich, I'm over here, come here…!" Instead of turning to greet him, Ulrich opened the door of the barracks forcefully and disappeared inside. Erhard stood another minute as if rooted in place, then approached the barracks with heavy steps. Upon arriving at the barracks, he stopped to wipe his brow, which was covered in sweat. In the hut into which Ulrich had just entered was a ping-pong table, on which two POWs were eagerly engaged in a game. Ulrich was not anywhere to be seen. Surprised, Erhard looked around and asked the two players: "Hey, didn't someone just come in here?" The two paused their game and one said: "Just now? No, we've been alone in here for quite a while." Shaking his head, Erhard left. "But that's impossible... he must..." Erhard mumbled to himself as he left the barracks.

A lot was going on in the canteen. Card players sat at every table and in the corner was someone playing the accordion. Ulrich Von Schütz was sitting at a table. He was wearing a dark blue PW shirt and holding up a Skat card he was about to slap forcefully onto the table. "Ulrich!" Erhard shouted, full of joy, "Hey, old buddy, there you are!" Whooping with joy, Ulrich stood up, threw his cards down, and flung himself at Erhard. After warm and loud greetings, Erhard, suddenly serious, asked him: "Say, weren't you just in the table tennis barracks at the front of the camp?" "No," Ulrich answered, "why do you ask? I've been playing Skat here for about two hours." "And," Erhard continued, startled, "do you still have your white bush shirt?" "No," answered Ulrich, subdued, "that had so many holes, blood and dirt spots on it I had to throw it away. Hey man, for God's sake, why are you asking me about that now?" "Never mind," Erhard replied, unsettled, "I'll explain some other time..."

9. Paranoia Persecutoria (Persecution Complex)

The morning after their reunion, Ulrich and Erhard met to discuss what had happened during the months of their separation. Ulrich's recovery took almost half a year; fortunately he had completely healed, with no lasting consequences from his many injuries. Only a few scars remained on his face as a permanent "souvenir" of what had happened.

Right after they started talking, Ulrich brought up a very serious subject, telling Erhard what he thought had happened to Hans Bergmann in the past two years. "Believe me, Erhard," he began, "he's definitely mentally confused. From what I know about neuroses or mental illness, I suspect he's suffering from a persecution complex. It's a strange story. He hasn't told you about his imagined gruesome experiences?"

"No, Ulrich, I was with him yesterday evening for the first time, and only for a short while. But I noticed his appearance. He looked like someone hunted, someone desperate."

"Yeah," Ulrich agreed, "that's it exactly. He feels like he's constantly being persecuted by all kinds of people. Of course none of it's true. He suspects everyone he comes in contact with. If you offer him a cigarette, he'll take it, but he won't smoke it, because he thinks it's poisoned. You know what? We'll check on him tonight; maybe we can help him somehow."

. . .

As Ulrich and Erhard entered the hospital that evening, Hans Bergmann had just finished working and was ready to relax in the nicely decorated quarters he shared with two other orderlies. Of course, it thrilled him to see his two old friends, but an unmistakable aura of grim mistrust emanated from him.

"Come on in," Hans said jovially, "and make yourselves comfortable. I don't even know how the past year was for you, Erhard. Won't you tell me about it?"

As requested, Erhard started talking, during which Hans twice interrupted by suddenly raising his hand, asking for quiet, and listening tensely as he opened the door to see if there was anyone outside. When he did this for no apparent reason a third time, his two friends asked him why he was so worried about people possibly listening in.

"Oh, you know," answered Hans excitedly, "my two roommates are very dangerous fellows. They're surely somewhere in the hospital, plotting again even now. Of course, they were unsuccessful in their first attack against me."

"Hey man," said Erhard, quite startled, "what nonsense are you talking? Why would they want to harm you?"

"Why?" Hans interjected, dejectedly putting his head in both his hands. "Why? If only I knew! But it's definitely not nonsense. You'll realize that right away when I tell you what happened to me a few days ago. So listen carefully. I'm lying in bed at night and I'm asleep. Suddenly, I'm woken up by a sharp pain in my left arm, and my eyes pop open. Petrified with fear, I see a shadowy figure in a nightshirt bending over me, pulling a hypodermic needle out of the crook of my left elbow. I start up and the figure jumps away and lies down in the bed over there. So it has to have been Christian Markert, since he sleeps there. Driven by a stinging pain in my arm, I climb out of bed, turn on the light, and look at the inside of my elbow. Sure enough, there's the stick of the needle: a tiny red dot. Frightened, I look in the mirror, and there — can you imagine? — the whites of my eyes are now completely red, blood red. Imagine how scared I was! As I then walk over to Christian's bed, the louse acts like he's sleeping, of course. His breathing is loud and gurgling, and, of course, there's no sign of the needle. He probably took it right into his bed. For days afterwards, I was weak and dizzy from that shot he gave me."

As he finished and stared straight ahead, shaking his head, Erhard and Ulrich exchanged a long glance. Then Erhard asked, "Tell me, Hans, has anything like that happened to you before? Has someone made an attempt on your life?"

"Oh, that's been going on for a long time," replied Hans resignedly. "There must be a bunch of them working together to get me out of the way. Imagine, just recently, someone attempted to poison me in a most ingenious way. Orderly Fritz Kranz, a very underhanded fellow, one day brought me a large tomato that he pressed upon me. He claimed it came right out of the icebox, was refreshing and delicious, and urged me to eat it right away. I saw him watching me covertly. I accepted the tomato, took it into the bathroom, and scrutinized it. As I suspected, there was a tiny needle hole. I broke the tomato in half at this spot—and look at that! — saw that the flesh was already all gray from the poison. Of course, I immediately threw the tomato into the toilet. As I looked up, my heart almost stopped with fright. The bathroom wall, made of horizontal wooden boards, had gaps of about two centimeters between the boards. And through one of these gaps, I could see two glittering eyes watching me closely. I immediately ran behind the wall, but only heard quick footsteps in the distance. Fritz, who wanted to watch me eat the poisoned tomato, had disappeared like a flash."

Exhausted, Hans fell silent, followed by another listening session. "Go look, Erhard," he cried out, "see if there's somebody outside. I think I heard Kube's voice." Obediently, Erhard opened the door, looked outside and closed it again. "There's nobody," he said comfortingly to Hans.

"You know," Hans continued quietly, as if he were telling a secret, "my other roommate, Erich Kube, is part of the conspiracy against me. Recently he gave me a gift of poisoned tobacco. You could already tell by the smell. To catch these two-bit murderers in the act for once, I gave the tobacco to the head doctor, Dr. Tulper, for analysis. He must be part of this crowd also, because when I asked him several days later what the results of the analysis were, he said with a mocking laugh he had smoked my poisoned tobacco and was still alive. I should rid myself of my preconceived notions! But he was probably well aware that people had been trying to do away with me for some time now. If I wasn't so attentive all the time, I would probably be six feet under by now."

Erhard Gast conducted a somewhat gruesome experiment with Hans. He pulled a pack of cigarettes out of his pocket in which there were still two cigarettes, put one between his lips, and offered the other to Ulrich. Then he laid the empty pack down in front of him, searched his pockets for a fresh pack, opened it, and hastily extended the full pack to Hans. Hans paused a moment before accepting. His glance flicked back and forth between the empty pack on the table and Erhard's and Ulrich's impassive faces. Then, whistling softly to himself, he carefully drew out a cigarette. As Erhard proffered a lighted match, he hastily waved him off, declaring emphatically: "I'll smoke this cigarette later...!"

.　　.　　.

"You don't know how grateful I am, Mr. Gast," said Dr. Tulper to Erhard. "Since you told me the story about the photo of Mrs. Monika, I understand the development of Bergmann's mental illness much better. That was the missing link for me. Now I know the source of his compulsion. This is the most severe case of paranoia persecutoria (persecution complex) that I have ever come in contact with here in captivity. I doubt if we can ever fully heal Bergmann."

"But doctor, can't you have him sent home immediately? Maybe being together with his wife again can heal his mind. Most likely, he will forgive her."

"Yes, if only one could know for sure if that is the cure," said Dr. Tulper thoughtfully. "But I agree with you: Maybe the return home will heal him. I will try to have him be the first one of us to return home. Unfortunately, he is not the only one to suffer psychological harm through being held in captivity." With alarm, Erhard Gast thought suddenly of his hallucination the night before: watching Ulrich enter the barracks wearing his white bush shirt, although this could have been none other than his "astral being," as the real Ulrich was actually in the canteen during this time. "Damn captivity," thought Erhard Gast sorrowfully. "It has messed all of us up."

10. Symphony

Slowly, the egg-shaped ferryboat pulled away from the pier in the New York harbor. Several thousand German prisoners sighed with relief, because this instant meant the end of a lengthy period in exile behind barbed wire, and maybe the end of being locked up altogether. Were they bound for England, France? Nobody knew, but all silently hoped that they were finally on their way home. Although the months spent in America were more than bearable, captivity had deprived them of the most precious human gift of all: freedom.

The ferryboat glided slowly over the gently rolling waters of the harbor. Dance tunes rang out from the loudspeakers, and the prisoners were in a festive travel mood. Erhard Gast and Ulrich Von Schütz stood up front in the boat's bow and were among the first to see the Statue of Liberty suddenly appear on their right from out of the water. Standing proudly on a small island, she triumphantly raised her torch of freedom into the air. To their left, the immense skyscrapers of the Manhattan peninsula rose steeply into the sky. Slow foxtrots and boogie-woogies accompanied all of this, streaming out of the loudspeakers, a scene that couldn't have been more American.

When the ferryboat was situated precisely between Manhattan and the Statue of Liberty, the wonder of the prisoners reached its apex. Erhard and Ulrich pensively regarded the colossal goddess with the halo crown. "Look, Ulrich," Erhard said thoughtfully, "this lady personifies freedom, one of the most beautiful, controversial and contradictory values of human existence. We know that too. Although we lived for two years in the land of the free, freedom was not within our reach. And now we still don't know if we are making our way towards freedom." "That's right," Ulrich countered, "no one knows if the proud, still woman over there is smiling at us disdainfully or promisingly. We want to inspect her carefully, though—the Statue of Liberty, America's pride!"

An American sailor from the boat's crew, who was standing with the prisoners in the bow, overheard these last few English words of Ulrich's. He approached the two of them slowly and said in his broad Flatbush accent: "Yeah, boys, our Statue of Liberty is very important to us. But believe me, freedom didn't just fall into our laps. We had to fight for it. And"—here he bent forward in a kindly, conspiratorial manner—"when you get back home and make certain that no new dictator comes to power, then you can finally fight for freedom too. Will you do that?" The two friends had to laugh, that such a good, simple man could, in just a few words, give them such valuable advice that they couldn't take seriously enough. "Sure, old friend," Erhard emphatically assured him, "this time we'll be very careful and stay away from a new dictator like the plague."

The sailor's eyes were damp with joy. The little mission he had undertaken, to caution gently the homeward-bound Germans, had met with success, and that did the modest man a world of good. He quickly offered a cigarette to each of them, patted them on the shoulder, and proclaimed warmly: "Good luck to you, friends. And don't forget the meaning of our Statue of Liberty!" Contentedly, he disappeared into the crowd.

Ulrich and Erhard looked at each other in amusement as they smoked their newly gained Chesterfields. A new song was emanating from the ship's loudspeakers: tender tones ringing forth, full of yearning. Astonished, the two friends listened as both their thoughts wandered back to Luc-sur-Mer and the Bar Américain. How often they had played and sung there together! And now they heard it once more, and a deep, female voice was singing, not the familiar French lyrics but English lyrics instead:

Symphony of love
Music from above

How does it start?
You walk in, and the song begins
Singing violins start in my heart
Then you speak, the melody seems to rise,
Then you sigh, it sighs and softly dies
Symphony, sing to me…

"Oh, Ulrich," Erhard cried out, flooded with happy memories, "how often we played that with old Jérôme, you at the piano and me on the drums, and also the last evening, only a few hours before the invasion began… Shortly after that Jérôme wanted to make us his prisoners. But when we weren't in agreement, he couldn't bring himself to shoot his two 'Symphony' players."

Grinning, he looked straight ahead as the ferryboat closed in on a large passenger steamboat, steam going, readying itself to take the prisoners to Europe. Once again, the melody wafted up. Sunk in thought, Ulrich's hands glided over the piano keys and Erhard sang along softly, as he strolled through the blooming garden of his memories:

Et j'entends, grande à l'infini
Comme une harmonie
Ma symphonie, ma symphonie…
(And I hear, great as all infinity
Like a harmony
My symphony, my symphony…)

Afterword

Some of those who were in the German military, and then in American captivity, will maintain that much of what is in my book could not possibly be true. But because I am expecting this reproach, I would like to address it briefly, so that those who have no way of verifying if the reports I give are true can decide whether to believe me or those who would criticize me.

Those who would claim, faced with their own experience, that my depictions are inauthentic, belong, in that which concerns their neutrality, to the "Africans"*. The "Normandists"* will only be able to confirm the truth of my reports. Yes, they will even sympathize with my shining an especially bright light upon certain truths in order to highlight them.

To give expression to these truths by shining a bright light on them is the goal of my book. If these accounts of my experiences work more in favor of the "Normandists" and against the prevailing "Africans", then they will have achieved their purpose.

*These expressions are to be understood only metaphorically!

The End

Notes on the Text: *Part 2: The Charybdis of the Barbed Wire*

1. Camp Aliceville In Alabama, USA

There were several German POW camps in Alabama, some permanent, some temporary. Including work camps, there were about 26, but Aliceville was by far the largest. My father often spoke of the good food he ate in Alabama, especially in contrast to the hunger he had experienced previously. Apparently, prisoners complained about the alleged inferiority of American white bread and coffee, though, and the camps tried to provide them with food more to their liking.

Many people don't realize that there were German prisoners of war throughout the United States in WWII, especially in the South: up to 425,000 German prisoners housed in 700 camps, in at least 46 states. Camp Aliceville was the largest of the POW camps in the Southeastern United States and had room for about 6000 prisoners, although there were not always that many at one time. The German prisoners at Camp Aliceville and at the other camps received humane treatment, partly in keeping with the Geneva Convention of 1929, partly because the United States government hoped that the German government would reciprocate in its treatment of American prisoners in Germany. The German prisoners recognized that the treatment in the United States was better than anywhere else.

Rail usually brought the prisoners to the camp, to the Aliceville train station on the Frisco line, and then they marched the couple of miles to the camp on the outskirts of town. It is impossible for me to say whether Erhard Gast's arrival by truck transport instead of by train is fiction or not.

2. Hans Bergmann Gets To Know His Wife

What I translated as "a sort of meal ticket relationship with no strings attached" was *ein Bratkartoffelverhältnis* in German, which literally means "fried potato relationship". It is slang for a loose, extra-marital, short-term love affair that takes place at the instigation of a man, primarily in exchange for home-cooked meals and other domestic comforts. Germans often use this expression together with *wilde Ehe* ("wild marriage"), a living-together relationship with a man that widowed women engaged in after the war in order to still draw their widow's pension.

This chapter gives reason to believe that Gast and Bergmann both lived in Compound A. But I believe that my father most likely lived in Compound E, as evidenced by certificates of study that I have from the camp school, signed by instructors in that compound. Compound E was the most undesirable, given that it was located the closest to the swamp at the back of the camp, in closer proximity to swarms of mosquitos, snakes and other undesirable wildlife. I will discuss the camp school program in more detail later.

At first, the Americans strictly separated prisoners from different compounds and did not allow them to visit each other. Later on, the prisoners could visit the other compounds for a few hours on Sundays. But by the time my father got there in the second half of 1944, prisoners could usually circulate more freely between compounds.

3. The Story Of The Bald Pate

The Geneva Convention of 1929 required that the United States provide the German prisoners of war with living quarters comparable to those of its own military; this mandate of equal treatment also meant being paid American military wages. Because American soldiers were being sent overseas, the resulting labor shortage meant that German POWs worked in canneries, mills, farms and other places deemed a minimal security risk. The minimum pay for an American enlisted soldier was 80 cents a day. Part of the prisoners' wages helped pay for the POW programs, and the workers could use the rest as pocket money for the camp canteen. According to Ulrich Von Schütz, this amounted to 10 cents a day, or $3.00 a month.

4. Now I Know What We Are Fighting For!

Construction workers completed Camp Aliceville in December 1942. By June 1943, it began receiving German POWs, at first mostly from the *Afrika Korps* of *Feldmarschall* Erwin Rommel, also known as *der Wüstenfuchs* (Desert Fox). These were the soldiers captured early in the war during Germany's greatest military successes (the "Africans" that Karlheinz refers to). Most of the devoted Nazis were among this group, and they harassed, injured or killed prisoners who they thought were identifying too much with their American captors. The "Normandists", those soldiers captured during the Battle of Normandy, like my father, had much more realistic views of the likely outcome of the war. The earlier prisoners from Rommel's *Afrika Korps* considered them traitors or deserters.

The American Office of the Provost Marshal General (OPMG), which supervised the German prisoner of war camps, began a formal reeducation program for German prisoners in the fall of 1944. It was called the Special Projects Division (SPD) and among other efforts published the newspaper *Der Ruf* (The Call) that Karlheinz refers to, a prison newspaper edited by sympathetic POWs. American university professors prepared the content of Der Ruf and it was essentially a literary journal with little current news; it did not appeal to most of the prisoners. There was another camp newspaper in Camp Aliceville, the weekly *Der Zaungast* (The Guest Behind the Fence), which was published by the prisoners themselves. The Aliceville Museum has copies of every issue published.

5. The Kangaroo Court

A "fifth column" is a group of people who undermine a larger group from within, usually in favor of the enemy group. "Defeatists" hold an ideological stance that actively considers cooperation with the enemy. In a military context, defeatism can be synonymous with treason. Hardcore Nazis in the camps sometimes attacked or killed those they had convicted of disloyalty in their kangaroo courts; these midnight beatings and killings were known as the "Holy Ghost". The Nazis accomplished the beatings and murders with bare hands, knives, iron bars, or even cooking utensils. Some prisoner "suicides" were likely murder.

6. The Most Beautiful Woman In The World

Officers were not required to work as per the Geneva Convention. At the end of the war, once Germany had surrendered, most prisoners were not immediately sent home like they expected and many continued working in the United States or Europe until 1946 or even 1947. As the Geneva Convention no longer applied once Germany had surrendered, and in retaliation for the atrocities discovered at the concentration camps, the camps cut prisoners' food rations and increased their workloads. As Karlheinz points out, most officers made a choice to work at the smaller work camps in return for more food and some meager pay.

7. Pitt Kisses Molly

The hospital and its corresponding German prisoner of war work camp that Karlheinz refers to was Northington General Hospital in Tuscaloosa, Alabama. Built as a temporary Army hospital during World War II, it no longer exists. (The language in this chapter is anything but "politically correct").

8. A Man Goes Into The Hut

This chapter shows the terrible mental toll two or more years of captivity had taken on the prisoners, which becomes even more apparent in the next chapter. The soldiers were now just waiting to be sent home. It turns out that some of them ended up in the United Kingdom or France, and some spent up to three more years as laborers there, arguably violating the Geneva Convention's requirement of rapid repatriation.

9. Paranoia Persecutoria (Persecution Complex)

Nowadays, we would say that Hans Bergmann was probably suffering from some form of PTSD, Post Traumatic Stress Disorder. We learn he is suffering from paranoia, which can be present in a persecutory delusional disorder. According to Gast and Von Schütz, however, he also exhibits symptoms of hypervigilance, which can be a component of PTSD but differs somewhat from paranoia. He is without a doubt a changed man because of his imprisonment.

10. Symphony

They sent my father to Liverpool, not Germany, in 1946 when they released him from Camp Aliceville. He and some prisoners like him, who were also "British-owned", went to Liverpool and had to remain in captivity in Britain for some time, where they were "de-Nazified" and given lessons in democracy. Germany repatriated them starting in September 1946, but I don't know the exact date in the fall when Karlheinz returned to his mother and sister in Bavaria. The earliest date on a letter sent to him at the first British camp where he was being held, addressed to POW Camp 189, Dunham Park, Altrincham, Cheshire, Great Britain, was April 29, 1946. The latest date was September 1, 1946, and he notes he received this letter on September 26, 1946. By this time, he was in a different British camp, POW Camp 271, at the RAF Airfield in Attleborough, Norfolk.

Afterword

Most of the most ardent Nazis in the German POW camps came from the ranks of Rommel's *Afrika Korps* and had been captured early in the war. Karlheinz seems to be quite circumspect in his criticism of the Nazis. He started writing this book in December 1947, only a year after his release. He may still have been reluctant to voice his opinions too freely for a lingering fear of retribution. In fact, my father never refers to Camp Aliceville or the town of Aliceville in his memoirs, maybe for the same reason; he calls it Camp Troy in Troy, Alabama. Troy was actually over three hours by car from Aliceville and there was only a small, temporary POW camp there. I have changed every mention of Camp Troy and the town of Troy to Camp Aliceville and the town of Aliceville for consistency's sake.

PART III: DOCUMENTING

You might wonder how I came to undertake this project of writing my memoir, incorporating my father's memoirs. By the end of 2018, I had finished typing both of Karlheinz's books and shared them with the German-speaking family members. My German aunt, *Tante* Maria (four years younger than her sister, my mother) liked them very much and said they brought back memories she had nearly forgotten.

I sent both books to a German literary agent, who said the writing style was beautiful, and she enjoyed reading them, but that World War II memoirs had saturated the market, and that too much time had passed for people to be interested in this type of material. In January 2019, I sent both books to some leading publishers in Germany, anyway. There was no interest in publication.

I then translated both books from German into English to share with the American family members and possibly pursue publication in the United States. Very few Americans know that there were German prisoner of war camps in the US, and I felt that there was some important information here that might be of interest. Again, family and friends enjoyed reading the books, so I followed up on some contacts I had with an agent and a publisher. There were some compliments on the books, but no interest in publication.

This is when I realized that World War II literature seems to fit into two general groups: what I will refer to as "Nazi-hunting and vilification" and "Holocaust literature". So either there are stories of combat, resistance and hunting down the enemy, or there are stories of endurance, suffering and survival. As one of my author friends put it, my father's books are the memoirs of the "universal soldier": of the petty injustices, minor triumphs, yearning for home and bonds of friendship experienced under the pressures of war. Also, I find my father's writings to be very lyrical, cerebral and intellectual. There is little overt violence or crudity, and no sex, as well as an absence of swashbuckling adventure. His writing style may have had more appeal to an audience of readers from 70 years ago than today. And anyway, is a German soldier under Hitler even entitled to a "universal" soldier's experience?

It was when my husband Harry, who was a Visiting Fellow at the Andlinger Center for Energy and the Environment of Princeton University, and I and were in Princeton, New Jersey at the end of 2019, that an esteemed memoir writer and professor of creative non-fiction suggested I write a memoir recounting how I discovered these books, and how they led me to a new understanding of my father.

I enrolled in a memoir-writing class at the Princeton Senior Resource Center at the beginning of 2020 and wrote the first few chapter drafts of this book as part of my class assignments. The class was enjoyable; the instructor was wonderful, and my classmates were encouraging. On the draft of my first chapter, the instructor commented, "An enchanted suitcase!" There was the title of my book.

If you are reading this and the year 2020 resonates with you, then you know exactly why I suddenly had the time to immerse myself fully in this project. We returned from Princeton to our home in Springfield, Virginia on March 1st, receiving lockdown, stay-at-home orders by the middle of March, because of the worldwide rampage of the coronavirus. I had been looking forward to resuming my profession as a tour guide in Washington, DC, and even squeezed in a few tours before everything shut down. Despite my best efforts to procrastinate, I suddenly had nothing to do but write.

I can only describe this entire process as a voyage of discovery, and the suitcase in the basement as truly enchanted. How many grown children get the chance to see their deceased parent in a whole new light? It was, in fact, an entirely new relationship with my father as far as I was concerned, albeit one-sided. I suddenly felt a curious sense of closeness with him from the vantage point of being almost the same age he was when he died, looking through a window that had unexpectedly opened up into the past.

I have gone into some detail about my process in order to inspire you, the reader. You might also have a cache of letters, papers or diary entries in a closet, basement or attic. Take a closer look: there might be an interesting story right under your very nose.

• • •

An admiration of all things American comes through clearly in Karlheinz's books, and indeed, he emigrated to the United States in 1951, to the Washington, DC area where his mother and sister were already living, once he had finished his German undergraduate law studies. In order to be admitted as an immigrant from Germany after the war, the United States required an American sponsor who would vouch for your character. The United States did not accept German immigrants at all immediately after the war, but this became possible a few years later. My father's sponsor was the US Army officer who he took his orders from at Camp Aliceville, Bob Hahnen from Minnesota. This officer did not enlist or get drafted into the Army until 1944, at the ripe old age of 37. They became good friends during their time together in Alabama and stayed in touch until Bob Hahnen's death, prior to that of my father.

Today there is a museum, the Aliceville Museum, opened in February 1995, in the former Coca-Cola Bottling Plant in Aliceville, Alabama. The Aliceville POW Camp Exhibit dedicates itself to the German prisoner of war camp that played such a prominent role in the town's history. In fact, the town of Aliceville hosted six reunions for the German prisoners, American military, and townspeople in 1989, 1993 (50th anniversary of the camp), 1995, 1999, 2001 and 2003 (60th anniversary). Unfortunately, my father died in 1986, three years before the first reunion. He would have loved to have attended that first reunion and subsequent ones as well. The current director of the museum, John Gillum, told me that the reunions are no longer being held because so few people from that time are still alive.

•   •   •

Among the letters that Karlheinz's friend Editha Sobbe returned to him were two letters to her from Karlheinz's mother, my grandmother Else Stoess. The first one dates from October 27, 1944. Karlheinz's capture took place eight days after D-Day, on June 14, 1944; by October, he had already been in the Aliceville POW Camp for several months. Else informs Editha of Karlheinz's capture: Editha knows something happened because an envelope postmarked June 6th (D-Day) addressed to Karlheinz came back to her, stamped "Whereabouts Unknown". What follows is my translation of the letters.

Else lets Editha know Karlheinz is doing well:

"Great joy has come to us amid our suffering. Karlheinz wrote to us from American captivity. He is in Alabama in North America; that's on the Gulf of Mexico. He seems to fare well, except for homesickness. There is everything you could think of: movies, a chapel, a library, academic courses, a camp newspaper, and sports fields. He wants to use this time to develop intellectually and to build his physical strength (the food also seems to be good) so that he will be ready for the arduous work after the war. He sends greetings to everyone who is asking about him, and also to you, dear Fräulein Sobbe, and would like us to write often, and a lot. I'm using this opportunity to give you his address, in case you can and have the time to write to him:"

Feldwebel Karlheinz STOESS 31 G 5060, Co. No. 20
Prisoner of War Camp Aliceville c/o G.P.O. Box 20
New York, N.Y., U.S.A.

She gives Editha instructions on writing letters to him:

"One can write to him once a week, one-sided preferred, using the Latin alphabet or typewritten, the address in block letters. On the envelope next to the address: By Airmail to North America, 40 Pfennig postage, and handed to the postal clerk (not deposited in the mailbox)."

By "Latin alphabet", Else means not the Old German "Kurrent" handwriting that is almost impossible to read unless you have learned to do so, and which was sometimes still in use during the World War II time period.

On November 9, 1944, Else writes to Editha again and gives further instructions for writing to Karlheinz:

"You've already written to Karlheinz? It will surely thrill him to get letters from home. His mail from Alabama to here (Dresden) took exactly 3 months. How long it takes to get to him, I don't know, but maybe the same number of months. One can only write about familiar things, namely nothing political. No postcards, no newspapers, shorthand, musical notes, incomprehensible abbreviations, excerpts or references to books or poems, or any references to wartime measures or to the economic and political situation; they don't allow newspapers or magazines. You may not number the letters. Write using the Latin alphabet (preferably with a typewriter), be short and to the point, and use only one side of the paper. Letters that are difficult to read don't make it past the censors. I'm sure you did it right. You may write once a week. The address has to be in block letters."

About two weeks after her first letter to Editha, Else writes:

"We have heard nothing further from Karlheinz. We hope, though, that he's faring well and that he will write to us again as soon as he can. The prisoners—specifically those in the USA—can write two letters and four postcards a month. Unfortunately, not all letters arrive; the censors destroy some of them because they're

unclear or difficult to read because of the handwriting, or they get lost. Eventually something slips through."

The front of the folder that Karlheinz kept his letters in has a stamp on it: "CENSORED: Fort Benning Internment Camp". Fort Benning Camp in Columbus, Georgia, was open from 1942 to 1946 and housed 2234 POWs. They may have initially processed the letters at Fort Benning before sending them on to Camp Aliceville.

In a letter dated December 1, 1944, written to her son, Karlheinz's mother informs him of some sad news:

"My dear Karlheinz!

So far, I have gotten one letter from you. I have answered it often. I hope that at least one of my letters has reached you. I have already let you know that your dear father received a promotion to senior executive officer in the government. That gave you much happiness, didn't it? He was also very pleased. Unfortunately, he can't enjoy his good fortune anymore. His illness was too heavy to bear. I already wrote to you in the summer that his condition was of concern, because a bout of pleurisy made it very difficult for him to breathe and led him to feel he was suffocating, forcing him back to his hospital bed. Now he is finally free of his suffering. On November 20th he lay down for his last rest, after having solemnly promised me he would return to me again. He thought he would not die of this illness. The dear Lord had other intentions and brought him home. Calmly and peacefully, he crossed to the other side without realizing that he was dying. Don't cry, my good boy. Life is hard, but it will find us to be even harder. I am strong enough to bear even this pain. You know me; if the wind is against me, I step into it all the more resolutely. I wait only for you and I know we will see each other again. Then everything will be good. I had many joys in my life. I had a happy marriage, could offer healthy, splendid children to the Fatherland, and never wanted for anything. Therefore, it is only right that I must give a good deal in return. I am still here for you and Ilse and will never abandon you. So, be brave.

Your loving mother."

One extremely interesting discovery I made was in a subsequent letter from her, dated January 2, 1945. She included the beginning of a letter that Karlheinz's father Rudolf had written to him before he died, and she quotes the following from his father's letter:

"*As that dear Michi informed us, and as we heard and read elsewhere, the little Distelfink* (goldfinch) *still chirped enthusiastically for 11 more days, before it lost its voice because of inadequate nourishment. The entire family rejoiced in its birdsong.*"

This was undoubtedly a coded reference to the military surrender after D-Day of the radar station—code-named *Distelfink* or "Goldfinch"—Karlheinz's posting on the Normandy coast.

Almost one-and-a-half years later Else sends Karlheinz a special postcard meant for soldiers, dated May 20, 1946, to a POW camp in Great Britain in Dunham Park, Altrincham, Cheshire, where Karlheinz had ended up after Aliceville, prior to his repatriation to Germany. Only next of kin can send this kind of postcard, and it can't contain over 25 words. It reads: "*We are alive and healthy. Have lost everything. We're waiting here for you. I need you urgently.*" She and Karlheinz's younger sister Ilse resettled as refugees in the town of Rehau in Bavaria, after bombs had destroyed their apartment building.

Else writes Karlheinz a regular postcard (not subject to the same military restrictions) the very next day, May 21, 1946:

"My dear Karlheinz!

Now you are closer to our homeland, which we no longer have. We have lost everything. We live here now and are waiting for you and I need you so badly. Ilse is an interpreter with the American military government in Rehau and I earn a few Pfennig with embroidery. Our quarters are small and shabby, but at least we have a roof over our heads. Our health is good, but we have gotten very thin. I have my slender young girl's figure again."

After his arrival in Liverpool, Karlheinz transferred to New Park at Dunham Massey, the park of a British country house that the British military had requisitioned. Towards the end of the war, authorities turned the camp over to housing German POWs. Skilled linguists interrogated the prisoners here and began the process of "de-Nazification", necessary to repatriate the prisoners back to Germany.

On June 10, 1946, Else writes Karlheinz a letter before his 26th birthday on July 1st:

"My dear Karlheinz!

Once again, the anniversary of the day comes when full of joy and hope, I gave you life. How happy we were then, your father and I, in our small, humble apartment on the Rübauerstraße. Every year increased in happiness and thriftiness. You were a healthy, sweet boy and gave us nothing but joy. We realized early on that you were very smart and had a good head on your shoulders. Therefore, we also had high expectations for your future and gave you the best education we could.

And now, my dear son? The worst of all wars has cut in half that ribbon of hope. Everything is gone that contentment and thrift have wrought, gone the homeland, gone father and brother. It has left only us two weak women, your sister and I, in our great poverty.

What would be my son if you were to come soon? You are my only support and, if God were to wish it, my only help. Your return from captivity will be such a gift to me and then we will have to start over again, from the very beginning, as we no longer own anything.

On the day of your birth, I will think even more about you and I have only one wish for you and me: that a stroke of luck sends you back to me soon and that you can find me.

Endure until then, and we'll also be brave.

I send you greetings full of love and warmth and with many kisses,

Your mother and sister."

On July 20, 1946, Else writes to Karlheinz again:

"My dear Karlheinz!

On July 1ˢᵗ I really concentrated hard on thinking about you, decorated your picture with flowers, and had already written you a birthday letter on June 10ᵗʰ. I hope you've received it in the meantime.

Today your sweet, long letter reached us and so did your two cards.

What our life is like? Poor and simple. I only earn money by doing embroidery, and Ilse has a job as an interpreter in the American military government, as I have often written to you. No one is with us; we are all alone, Ilse and I.

What does Rehau look like? A small town, not much going on. We also don't want to stay here, but would rather settle in a big city, but only when you're here. Are you coming soon? The three months of your rebuilding work in England are almost over, right?

You have obviously informed yourself as to exactly where Rehau is located. That's correct.

We could really use groceries, because we often go hungry. I thank you for your efforts in advance.

On March 20, 1945, we evacuated to Bavaria. This is where our journey from town to town began, until we reached Rehau on September 1ˢᵗ, 1945, where we still live, although already in the third apartment.

But because I haven't lived here for a full year yet, I couldn't vote."

Else writes about mutual acquaintances and to inform him that two of his aunts, as well as many, many other people they knew, lost their lives during the bombing. She adds a PostScript: *"How happy I am to be in contact with you again after all this time!"*

In her letter dated July 23, 1946, Else tells her son about the bombing of Dresden twice in one night, the night of February 13, 1945, towards the end of the war:

"It is truly miraculous that we could escape with our lives from the hell we were in. As the building collapsed around us and those buried in the rubble were crying out for help, with the destruction barring all the emergency exits, I truly thought my last hour had come. Frau Becker (a friend of both Karlheinz's and his mother's) was very brave. We two left the bomb shelter last to save those who were crying out for help, and we didn't leave until we had rescued all the living, nine people, from the stones and rubble. We had to leave the three dead behind. Unfortunately, also one living. Our arms were too weak to lift the heavy stones off of Fräulein Tannenhauer; everything had to be accomplished in pitch darkness and we two women were all alone. All the other inhabitants of the apartment building had brought themselves to safety in the meantime, without heeding the cries for help.

The same night, we withstood the second bomb attack, in the street Deutsche Kaiser-Allee, in Herr Brause's apartment house. That building caved in also and we had to flee again through the flames to find another shelter. First, we went to the Elbe River to fill our lungs with some fresh air. Here we escaped death for yet a third time, as almost all of those who gathered there were killed, either shot or burned to death by low-flying planes.

We spent the rest of the night at a first aid station in Blasewitz, where we administered first aid to the suffering. It was awful, the moaning and weeping of the wounded and those who were crying out for their family members. I will never forget this night for the rest of my life. Here again, Frau Becker assisted energetically.

The saddest part of this entire tragedy was that Ilse was not with us. She had gone to the circus; a bomb had squarely hit it, and it was now just a heap of rubble. I never thought I would see my daughter Ilse again. After three days of searching, I found her in a half-destroyed building on Heubauer Street, beset by angina and smoke poisoning. How I thanked God that I had her with me again!

Now we are here in Rehau. Ilse has become a truly beautiful young woman; she will amaze you. She wants to move to America, to Michigan. An American is head over heels in love with her and wants her to come to him. We'll see what happens."

Ilse's Michigan admirer never responded to her many letters, and at the tender age of 18, she ended up marrying her American military boss from Rehau and moving to a farm in Lucketts, Virginia, with her mother in tow. She had stopped going to school at age 16 to work in the American military government in Rehau, thanks to her English skills. Apparently her English accent was so good that people sometimes mistook her for an American. I remember her soft southern accent with the barest hint of German.

My grandmother Else, whom I called "Mimi" to distinguish her from "Oma", my mother's mother, died in 1981 at age 86, after 10 years in a nursing home in Leesburg, Virginia following a broken hip. I admired her immensely for her many skills: painting, sewing, cooking, and fixing things that were broken. I always enjoyed spending time with her in the summers when I was young. However, I am even more full of admiration for her after reading her letters to my father, which I find almost unbearably touching. You can clearly tell what an affectionate relationship she has with her son. She misses him terribly and pours out her love for him in eloquent prose. In some letters, the censors had crossed out certain words with heavy black pen or even cut them out with scissors. My husband pointed out that some things she wrote about, like offering "healthy, splendid children to the Fatherland", may have been for the benefit of the censors.

Else endured so much, but I never saw her feeling sorry for herself or lamenting her fate. I now see that she was also an excellent wife and mother, besides being a loving grandmother. I wish I had spent more time with her while she was still alive. My sister and I called her "Mimi" (a name I came up with when I was a baby) but our cousins, *Tante* Ilse's four children, called her "Omi". Omi is the name I chose when I became a grandmother, in homage to her.

How hard it must have been for Karlheinz to read the letters about his father suffering from tuberculosis in the clinic, his mother's yearning for her husband to return to her, and his father's eventual death at age 50. This death followed hard on the heels of that of Karlheinz's brother Siegfried, just 21 years old, in the heat of battle on the dreaded Russian Front from which very few soldiers returned alive. At age 24, Karlheinz had already lost half his family as he sat helplessly behind barbed wire in a foreign land.

Among his papers was a letter carefully sealed in two envelopes that Karlheinz had written to be given to his parents in the event of his death. He thanked his parents for the kind and caring upbringing they had given him and how they had gently protected the sensitive and easily hurt child he was. I remember well the devotion he showed his mother as she lay sick and dying in the nursing home in Virginia. He would spend entire days at her bedside, unaware that he would die himself a mere five years later, when I was 29 years old.

Some time had passed, and it was now August 2021. The coronavirus had become less of a danger for vaccinated people, but it was still prevalent and still a problem. My mother had since died, on April 2, 2021, just a few months shy of her 100th birthday. The official cause of death was arteriosclerotic disease, but it was really just old age. It comforts me to know she had the chance to read my father's memoirs, and that we could discuss them with each other.

My mother had the great good fortune, at the very end of her life, to live with my daughter Macy and her husband Brendan on the farm where they lived with residents with disabilities. She got tremendous joy from being taken care of and visited by family, especially from being able to spend time with her first great-grandchild, Marcello Alfons, the son of my son Cliff and his wife Lola. While settling Irene's estate, I could closely scrutinize her files of documents from the war and beyond. I saw that her wartime and post-war life was just as interesting as my father's—living and studying all over Europe, the United States and Canada as a young German civilian—and realized that she could easily be the subject of her own book. I am determined that she will be.

I also found among my mother's possessions a file of letters that she had written to her mother Therese and sister Maria in Germany during the time she lived in Paris. The letters span nine years, from 1976 to 1985. They end with her mother Therese Misslbeck's death in 1985 at 93. Her family returned the letters to my mother after my grandmother's death. There was only one letter written by my father, in response to a letter from his mother-in-law following the death of his own mother in 1981. He sums up his mother's life succinctly in the translation of the German letter that follows:

Italy, June 16, 1981

Dear Therese,

Your letter, in which you express your condolences in response to the death of my mother, has done me a lot of good. When I saw her in February for several days once again (and when she could no longer speak) she suddenly embraced me and took leave of me forever. She knew we would not see each other again.

Her death was hard and full of pain. There were never any simple solutions for my mother. Torment clouded everything. The terribly long time in the nursing home was awful for her. But there was no other solution. My sister couldn't take care of her. Unfortunately, she couldn't visit my mother often or long enough, either. To compensate, I spent many weeks in the nursing home. Whenever I was in America, I stayed with my mother from morning until evening. We talked, told each other funny stories, and I pushed her in a wheelchair around the facility, as well as in the small town of Leesburg, where we visited the drugstore, the supermarket and even the local museum. Those were wonderful times for her. When I came back to my sister's in the evening, I was totally exhausted. These days were incredibly difficult for me. Once I fell asleep as I was sitting in a chair across from my mother. When I woke up, I saw her wide-open eyes fixed intently on me. She was just never tired when I was with her.

You're right, dear Therese. Her life was full of sacrifice. When my brother fell at age 21, she had to give support to my father, broken by this outcome. He had died already by age 50 and then she was alone. Bombs had destroyed Dresden, and she had to flee the city. When I saw her again in the fall of 1946, she had been almost entirely hollowed out. After that, she was mostly in tears. Nothing was right anymore. She was on her way to the end.

My dear Therese, thank you again for your condolences,

Your Karlheinz

There was one important thing I still needed to do: visit the German Prisoner of War Exhibit at the Aliceville Museum in Aliceville, Alabama. Would I find something that tied everything together?

The trip on August 19, 2021, did not start out auspiciously. It was my husband's and my first plane flight since the onset of the pandemic. Our late evening flight was further delayed by a couple of hours and we did not get to Birmingham, Alabama until almost midnight. After a few hours of restorative sleep in our charming bed-and-breakfast, we set out on the two-hour drive to Aliceville.

At the Aliceville Museum, we received a royal welcome from the director, John Gillum, with whom I had been corresponding for over a year. He loves to have families of former POWs visit and made us feel instantly welcome. We showed each other various photos and artifacts, and the chair of the museum board, Everett Owens, came to meet us. Later, they took us for a down-home lunch at Angie's Place, where Everett's son served us. He occasionally helps at the museum on Saturdays. Aliceville is like stepping back in time to small-town America, full of friendly people who all know each other.

We spent several hours poring over the fascinating, comprehensive exhibits about the camp. A very well done short video serves as an introduction to the exhibit and there are many artifacts donated by the prisoners, the townspeople and the various Military Police Escort Guard companies that served there. There are copies of every issue of the camp newspaper, *Der Zaungast* (The Guest Behind the Fence), that the prisoners published themselves on their own printing press. We also enjoyed the well-stocked gift shop and could have spent much more time at the museum.

I was hoping to find something that would tie everything together—a photo, a mention of my father's name—a smoking gun, of sorts. This did not happen, but something much more important did: I realized that there is an entire community, both local and international, that cares deeply about this history and works very hard to keep it alive and relevant. Alabama is justifiably proud of the fact that its citizens treated the German prisoners of war humanely, with dignity and respect. The sincere affection and fond memories that the former prisoners and the townspeople still harbor bear witness to this, as does the Germans' willingness to travel great distances for reunions with their former American prison guards.

John Gillum kindly provided us with an introduction to a prominent local author, Ruth Beaumont Cook, who has written the definitive history of the Aliceville Camp and the service of the townspeople during World War II: *Guests Behind the Barbed Wire: German POWs in America: A True Story of Hope and Friendship*. This beautifully written, comprehensive account (almost 600 pages) was of tremendous help to me as I was finishing this memoir, filling in gaps in my knowledge and confirming some of my father's observations. I also benefitted a great deal from the book compiled and edited by historian E.B. Walker, *A Brief History of Prisoner of War Camp Aliceville*. Both books were invaluable to me in helping me understand my father's place in this greater history. They are also part of a much larger canon of books about German prisoners of war in America. It is worth emphasizing once again how few Americans know anything at all about this significant facet of World War II.

• • •

Another surprise awaited me when I returned home a few days later. I was looking through my father's files for something else entirely, when I happened across two certificates of study from the German Prisoner of War School at Camp Aliceville. I translated them into English and have reproduced them here in their entirety:

German Prisoner of War School
Camp Aliceville, Alabama, USA

Certificate of Studies Nr. 194
According to Order OKW2F 24.30c pertaining to Prisoners of War -III-
Nr. 4407/42 of June 30, 1942

For the Fall Trimester from September 1 to December 23, 1944
NCO Feldwebel (technical sergeant) Karlheinz Stoess, born July 1, 1920 in Dresden, regularly attended courses offered by the camp school, under individually verified participation.

Chosen Field of Studies: Law and Economics

Chosen Courses:
    Civil Law
    Criminal Law
    Economics
    German Studies
    British Studies
    American Studies

Individual verification of the regularly attended lectures, study groups, seminars and practical assignments, with the following specifications:

Title/name of the lecture, study group, seminar, or assignment. Number of hours per week; course content; instructor qualifications.

The signature of the instructor confirms the entries.

• • •

<u>Lecture on Civil Law</u> (4 hours per week):

Overview of Civil Law with written assignments (I hour per week)
Signed by NCO Richard Ernst
Doctor of Law, District Judge
Obermoschel, Westmark

• • •

<u>*Lecture on Criminal Law*</u> *(2 hours per week):*

Overview of criminal law, history, interpretation and scope of criminal law; system of penalties and methods of securement; characteristics of offenses; causal relationships; types of offenders; illegality and corresponding exclusions.

Signed by NCO Johannes Graumann
Doctor of Law, District Judge
Schoenigen, Braunschweig

• • •

<u>*Lecture on Economics*</u> *(2 hours per week):*

History of Economics

Signed by NCO Philipp Oberle
Doctor of Economics, Tenured Secondary School Teacher
Heidelberg, System 18

• • •

<u>*Study Group for German Studies*</u> *(2 hours per week):*

Focus of studies: The German Novella from Goethe to the present.

Discussion of the novellas, with individual presentations on the life and work of the authors.

Goethe: Novelle; Kleist: Marquise of O.; Eichendorff: Taugenichts (Good for Nothing); Droste: Judenbuche (The Jew's Beech); Moerike: Mozart auf der Reise nach Prag (Mozart on the Journey to Prague); Stifter: Brigitta; Keller: Romeo und Julia auf dem Dorfe (A Village Romeo and Juliet); Heyse: L'Arrabbiata; Storm: Immensee und Schimmelreiter (Immensee and the Dykemaster); Raabe: Die Schwarze Galeere (The Black Galley); Fontane.

Signed by NCO Feldwebel (technical sergeant) Karl Schmidt
Teacher
Hamburg 20, Knauerstr. 22

• • •

<u>Study Group for British Studies</u> (2 hours per week):

Focus of studies: Prose during the time of Queen Elizabeth. Discussion of text excerpts from Woods-Watt-Anderson: "The Literature of England", N.Y., 1936, with individual presentations about the life and work of the authors.

Sir Thomas More: Utopia; Roger Ascham: The Schoolmaster; William Painter; Sir Walter Raleigh; Sir Philip Sidney; John Lyly; Euphues; Sir Edmund Spenser; Michael Drayton; Robert Greene; Thomas Dekker; Ben Jonson; Beaumont and Fletcher; Christopher Marlowe; William Shakespeare: Biography, Venus and Adonis, Sonnet. ("Forster", crossed out).

Signed by NCO Wachtmeister (technical sergeant) Hans Stuedl
Doctor of Philosophy, Tenured Secondary School Teacher
Wien (Vienna) II, Untere Augartenstr. 1

• • •

Study Group for American Language and Culture (2 hours per week):

Focus of studies: Phonetics according to Kenyon, language particularities taken from selected chapters of H. L. Mencken's "The American Language", N.Y., 1937. Overview of prose until approximately 1850, with individual presentations about John Smith, Cotton Mather, Philip Freneau, Benjamin Franklin, Thomas Paine, William Cullen Bryant, Washington Irving, James Fenimore Cooper; The Transcendentalists: Ralph Waldo Emerson. Also, an introduction to geography, history, the Constitution and education in the United States.

Signed by NCO Wachtmeister (technical sergeant) Hans Stuedl
Doctor of Philosophy, Tenured Secondary School Teacher
Wien (Vienna) II, Untere Augartenstr. 1

. . .

The simultaneous deployment of NCO Feldwebel (technical sergeant) Karlheinz Stoess as an instructor in the camp school for English in an evening course of 3 hours a week is hereby certified by the Head of Instruction for Compound E.

Signed by NCO Feldwebel (technical sergeant) Heinrich Gross
Teacher
Leihgesten bei Giessen

. . .

Aliceville, Alabama, January 22, 1945
Signed by Leutnant Wilhelm Westhoff,
Director of Studies

Tenured Secondary School Teacher
Duesseldorf, Vinckenstr. 6
Stamped with the signature of Hauptfeldwebel (Senior NCO) and
camp spokesman Johannes Bogdan
Prisoner of War Camp Aliceville
C/o Box 20, G.P.O. New York, N.Y., U.S.A.
(End of Certificate of Studies Nr. 194)

German Prisoner of War School
Camp Aliceville, Alabama, USA

Certificate of Studies Nr. 121
According to Order OKW2F 24.30c pertaining to Prisoners of War-III-
Nr. 4407/42 of June 30, 1942

For the Winter Trimester from January 1 to March 28, 1945

NCO Feldwebel (technical sergeant) Karlheinz Stoess, born July 1, 1920 in Dresden, applied for remote enrollment on January 10, 1945.
His application and a letter dated January 22, 1945, were directed to the German Red Cross.
He regularly attended courses offered by the camp school, under individually verified participation.

Chosen Field of Studies: Law and Economics

Chosen Courses:
    Civil Law
    Criminal Law
    Economics
    British Studies
    American Studies
    German Studies

Individual verification of the regularly attended lectures, study groups, seminars and practical assignments, with the following specifications:
Title/name of the lecture, study group, seminar, or assignment.
Number of hours per week; course content; instructor qualifications.

The signature of the instructor confirms the entries.

• • •

<u>Lecture on Civil Law</u> *(4 hours per week):*

Legal obligations, the General Part of German law, with written assignments.

Signed by NCO Richard Ernst
Doctor of Law, District Judge
Obermoschel, Westmark

• • •

<u>Lecture on Criminal Law</u> *(2 hours per week):*

Overview of Criminal Law: Fault; grounds for exclusion from liability; error; attempt and completion of the act; complicity, incitement, aiding and abetting; concurrence of offenses in one act, multiplicity of offenses, concurrence of laws; treating a series of violations as a single offense.

Signed by NCO Johannes Graumann
Doctor of Law, District Judge
Schoenigen, Braunschweig

• • •

<u>Lecture on Economics</u> *(2 hours per week):*

Theoretical economics: Research methods, basic concepts, economic theories, production factors, the transportation economics cycle.

Signed by NCO Philipp Oberle
Doctor of Economics, Tenured Secondary School Teacher
Heidelberg, System 18

•   •   •

Study Group for British Studies (2 hours per week):

Theme: British prose in the 17th and 18th centuries with text excerpts from Woods-Watt-Anderson: "The Literature of England", N.Y., 1936. Individual presentations given on John Donne, Robert Herrick, Sir John Suckling, John Milton, John Bunyan, Samuel Butler, Daniel Defoe, Jonathan Swift.

Signed by NCO Wachtmeister (technical sergeant) Hans Stuedl
Doctor of Philosophy, Tenured Secondary School Teacher
Wien (Vienna) II, Untere Augartenstr. 1

•   •   •

Study Group for American Language and Culture (2 hours per week):

Focus of studies: Overview of prose through individual presentations about Henry David Thoreau, Nathaniel Hawthorne, Edgar Allan Poe, Herman Melville. Additional presentations on American advertising, including via broadcast; sports in America; the American Civil War; the settlement of the Mississippi basin, of the Delaware, of the Hudson, and of Alaska; as well as geographical film documentaries about America.

Signed by NCO Wachtmeister (technical sergeant) Hans Stuedl
Doctor of Philosophy, Tenured Secondary School Teacher

Wien (Vienna) II, Untere Augartenstr. 1

• • •

Study Group for German Studies (2 hours per week):

1. *The German novella from Goethe to the present (continuation and conclusion of the subject from the fall trimester). Discussion through individual presentations given on the life and work of the authors of these and other novellas. C.F. Meyer: Gustav Adolf's Page; Hermann Hesse: Der Zyklon (Zyklon B Gas); G. Binding: Die Waffenbrüder (Brothers in Arms); G. Britting: Die Base aus Bayern (The Female Cousin from Bavaria). Overview of the creation of novellas in the present.*

2. *The German comedy, as shown through individual presentations: Provenance and historical development of comedies from antiquity through Lessing. G.E. Lessing: Minna von Barnhelm (Minna from Barnhelm); H. Von Kleist: Der zerbrochene Krug (The Broken Jug). Continuation of this subject in the next trimester.*

NCO Feldwebel (technical sergeant) Karl Schmidt
Teacher in Hamburg 20,
Knauerstr. 22

• • •

Aliceville, Alabama, March 28, 1945

Signed by Leutnant Wilhelm Westhoff
Director of Studies
Tenured Secondary School Teacher
Duesseldorf, Vinckerstr. 6

Stamped with the signature of Hauptfeldwebel (Senior NCO) and camp spokesman Johannes Bogdan
Prisoner of War Camp Aliceville
C/o Box 20, G.P.O. New York, N.Y., U.S.A.

•　　•　　•

Remarks:

An intermediary examination in keeping with the Presidium's Circular of the German Red Cross of May 19, 1944 S-Gr/Kr., Section B, or Circular Nr. 14 of the Swiss Consulate/Department of German Interests of October 25, 1945, was administered, pertaining to the "Code of German Civil Law, Contractual Obligations Law, General Part of German Law".

Signed by NCO Richard Ernst
Doctor of Law, District Judge
Obermoschel, Westmark

Aliceville, March 28, 1945
Wilhelm Westhoff, Director of Studies

(End of Certificate of Studies Nr. 121)

It is fascinating to see what the prisoners studied and which books they read, especially regarding American language and culture. Karlheinz attended the camp school from September 1, 1944, to March 28, 1945. I am not sure if he attended any courses after that; I know they transferred him to a work camp around the middle of 1945, when Camp Aliceville was being dissolved.

After the second trimester, he took a German law exam and applied for remote study credit through the German Red Cross. I don't have written confirmation that these credits were granted, but I remember my mother telling me that the University of Erlangen accepted the credits, allowing Karlheinz to continue his law studies, since he had already passed the first required exam. This confirms the fact that these were rigorous courses of study and that they held the students to high performance standards.

John Gillum let me know the museum did not have any certificates of study in their collection and that these were extremely helpful, informing the museum of the content of the course material and who taught the courses. He mentioned that they even had one textbook mentioned in the certificates.

•   •   •

Because I had found these valuable documents, I made one last pass through my father's papers to see if I could find anything else of interest that I might have missed. To my great surprise, I found the copy of a letter he had written in English to "Bill", who I believe was American Bill Rowe, a friend of his from his first years in Washington. Karlheinz wrote the letter, dated December 30, 1985, 10 months before his death on October 31, 1986, when he had already received a diagnosis of cancer and knew that he did not have long to live.

Paris, December 30, 1985

Dear Bill,

As you can see, I have followed your advice and have written down some of my thoughts. The whole thing is rambling and informal, but I did not have the energy to do it more methodically.

This is not to be destroyed at any event. I would even be glad if more than two people could read it. My thoughts about democracy, war, strikes, and terrorism occupy me constantly and force themselves out of me. I cannot look at an airline or railroad strike without being provoked. Unfortunately, not many people (actually very few) feel as strongly as I do.

Thoughts at age 65

1946—I am coming home to Germany after two years in Allied Prisoner of War camps. There is freedom in the air in Bavaria in spite of US Military Govt. trying to be tough. The US is opening centers for newly founded parties. What to do with the Communists? The US opens centers for this "democratic" party too.

1948—The hunger ends. Slowly, normal life begins again. Nobody wants back Nazi dictatorship. Democracy is accepted. Everything is improving, but slowly.

After having studied law under great hardship, I emigrate to the US in 1950. War in Korea. What for? There are many questions. American rigidity bothers me (this happens again years later during the war in Vietnam). I stick my neck out, criticizing our exposure there. This, however, does not do me any good with my peers.

In 1968, the US company for which I work sends me to France. I am very pleased. Some of the problems, which existed in

1946 in Europe, have not been solved. NATO is still there. We say we are ready to defend ourselves and our democracy. But are we? Russia is becoming stronger and more threatening. There is terrorism everywhere. What we need are evidently special laws to deal with terrorism. But nothing like this is forthcoming. We rather accept endless carnage than bending the rule of the law in a case where this is truly necessary.

Where to go from here? There is decadence all around us. Young people en masse who have no social conscience, no readiness to fight if necessary. "Why don't they kick in our rotten door?" somebody asks. It is quite true.

Still, I believe in democracy. People say with democracy we must accept things like organized crime, terrorism, "crime in the streets", a general state of insecurity, etc. All this I don't believe. I think democracy with teeth in it is possible and the only worthwhile political system.

I remember the entire Third Reich (in 1933, when its 12-year run began, I was 13). The very few things that were good in this state were all overshadowed by atrocious things: the knock at the door at 5 in the morning, concentration camps filled with innocent people (this imprisonment—illegal and arbitrary—was called "Schutzhaft" or "protective custody"), suppression of one freedom after another, and a murderous, aggressive war, waged without any need whatsoever.

Democracy is automatically for peace. This is still a hope for me, because if another Korea or Vietnam comes along, we may decide for the sake of our own peace not to get involved again. Why should we do so unless being directly threatened?

So I still have some hope for what Churchill said: "Democracy is the worst form of government, except for all the others." But what I want and demand is democracy with teeth in it. If nothing is regulated and done with determination, then everything collapses and the ruthless ones will overrun us. We should begin with fighting terrorism in an effective way. Of the enthusiasm I had for Democracy in 1946, nothing much is left at this time.

Now let me look back to my hometown Dresden between 1920 (the year of my birth) to 1939, the year I was drafted into the "Arbeitsdienst" (compulsory work service). There, I was selected to be sent to Nuremberg, to the "Parteitag des Frieden" (Party Day of Peace) to march before the Fuehrer with the Arbeitsdienst. However, this Parteitag never takes place because Hitler starts his war against Poland before the set date. Shortly after the beginning of the war, we leave our camp and build roads in Poland. At the end of 1939, we are all sent home. Only the shadows of war are now left in Poland. The Poles are totally crushed.

In 1940: The Army (in my case, Air Force Communications). Instead of too much drilling, there is training for becoming a telex operator (learning the touch system). In the summer, transfer to the West. Work as a teletypist in occupied France. The French have a certain humor, even in their predicament. I like them a lot better than many of the fellow Germans who surround me. There is also—in spite of the jackboot on their necks—a certain atmosphere of freedom. It affects me strongly. In a strange way, I am happy in France, even in my sinister role.

1944: The Invasion: two weeks of hell. At the end, many dead, the others prisoners of war. The treatment is correct. Voyage by convoy to the US. Attempts are made there to convince us that democracy is better than what we had (with mixed results).

One small event which showed me I had come to another world was this: while entering our first Prisoner of War Camp in Alabama, we were each given a handbill which started with the words "To my dear brothers, the prisoners of war." Actually: "An meine lieben Brüder, die Kriegsgefangenen." The comforting message under this address came from the Pope and gave me the feeling that life would indeed go on for us. It did.

I have to go back to Dresden where I was born and lived until I was drafted into the Arbeitsdienst (1939) and subsequently the army (at war, 1940). School was nondescript, boring and rather cruel. No pleasant memories. But I had my parents. They put a smile on my face as only they could. My mother lived for her three children, uneducated really, but very intelligent.

I would have liked to follow a professional career staying in Dresden (now DDR). Little did I know before 1939 that there would be no hope for this after the war, unless I decided to live with the Communists. So Dresden is a memory, one of the best I have. I had the privilege to live in one of the most beautiful cities in the world for 18 years.

The German Army deserves another comment. I entered naively, being friendly to everybody around me. It didn't help much. Those of lesser education were awful. Sergeants and officers were often beasts. How I would have loved to leave the cause in Hitler's war! But there was no realistic possibility for that. Those who deserted, usually for reasons of conscience, were caught and executed. Not a desirable prospect.

Strange, how democracy is my No. 1 topic in this writing. I love its principles and remember so well how different the opposite (dictatorship) is. I was only 18 when I made a remark in public (1939), which was critical of the Nazis. Somebody overheard me and had me arrested. I talked myself out of it but never forgot the feeling of horror.

I have to come back to the war. How can I pass it by so easily? An Englishman once told me, "Don't worry, it may never happen." Well, how few of us can follow such good but unemotional advice. Example: we had old men (over 55) in our strongpoint in Normandy in 1944, who had been sent there for guard duty. When the invasion came closer, these men wanted to go back to avoid dying in this forthcoming bloody event. Their wish was granted, and they hopped on a truck, feeling sorry for the 200 of us left behind. There were American and British fighter planes flying around all the time and shooting at everything that moved. They spotted the truck on its drive to the hinterland and did not stop firing into it for a long time. Not one of the "old men" survived, but most of the 200 left behind did and became prisoners of war.

One sees such a case and realizes that our life is in God's or Fate's hands. Here is another example from the war. When our strongpoint was still surrounded by the British, I inspected one of our trenches. A British tank gunner in the nearby woods spotted me and fired a grenade at me. It exploded above my head at the upper edge of the trench. I fell to the ground and crawled back as fast as I could. Full of splinters? Not one had hit me. At the same time, a dead comrade was carried into the bunker. Cause of death? A tiny splinter had entered his spine.

I cannot leave democracy without referring to something else. The most obnoxious right under it is the right to strike, particularly in public services which are constantly needed. How could it come to those abuses? Here in France, for example, the strike situation amounts to complete anarchy. In the US, it is bad too. I think of the air controllers' strike held in spite of the fact that they had all signed not to strike. Even the postal services (although they have the same restriction) were ready to strike. Since it was not so easy to fire all the striking postal employees, the culprits were placated by giving them what they wanted. I desire to see the right to strike banished. To me, it is not part of democracy. As it is now, millions of people can be held hostage by strikes in our countries. Yet, what do I see? In the press or in public discussion, I don't find a single voice saying what I feel so strongly. So how can we ever get rid of constant strikes, which do nothing but heat up inflation and anarchy?

Karl Stoess

• • •

It is striking that so much of this letter is about the long ago past, particularly the war. As I have already pointed out, the war was Karlheinz's chief preoccupation for the rest of his life. He omits any mention of his wife and two children. Karlheinz knew he was dying: he had had an operation to have a brain tumor removed, a complication of his Non-Hodgkin lymphoma, in October of that year. He wanted to know how much time he had left and the doctor told him two years (it would be only one). My father unwittingly gave me the gift of a summary of his life with this letter, confirming much of what I have written in these pages. I am so very grateful for this entire experience.

• • •

My takeaway from all of this is that my father's memoirs, letters and documents will have an important role to play in the museum's collections; I am therefore donating them. The museum has diaries kept by the prisoners and correspondence written and received by them, but here is an eyewitness account, revealing what daily life was like and what sorts of thoughts preoccupied the prisoners.

Five years have passed since I began working on this project, and sometimes I felt as if I was the only one interested. I don't feel that way anymore, however, having discovered an entire community of people who are very much interested. This project kept me going during the darkest days of the covid pandemic and gave meaning and shape to an otherwise formless and constantly shifting time.

I have new insight into my father's personality, motivations, and what his life was like before I was born. Even though Karlheinz died over 35 years ago, when I was almost exactly the same age as he was when he wrote his memoirs, I feel almost closer to him than when he was alive. What a stroke of luck, to get a second chance to know my father better, and by extension myself.

And last of all, we have a new granddaughter, Adalie Therese. She is the daughter of our daughter Macy and her husband Brendan, Marcello's little cousin. So this is also for the new generation and the generations to come—that they may never forget.

ABOUT THE AUTHOR

Nik Moghadar – Old Town Photo

Helga Warren is a Washington, DC tour guide specializing in German and French tours of the city, and a former public school German Immersion teacher. She lives in the Virginia suburbs of the nation's capital with her husband.

The daughter of two German parents, she grew up in a German-speaking household and had the good fortune of spending her teenage years in Paris, which led to lifelong involvement with languages.

Her grandchildren are the light of her life.

She would never have written a book if it weren't for that old suitcase.

NOTE FROM THE AUTHOR

Word-of-mouth is crucial for any author to succeed. If you enjoyed *The Enchanted Suitcase*, please leave a review online—anywhere you are able. Even if it's just a sentence or two. It would make all the difference and would be very much appreciated.

Thanks!
Helga Warren

We hope you enjoyed reading this title from:

BLACK ❦ ROSE
writing™

www.blackrosewriting.com

Subscribe to our mailing list – *The Rosevine* – and receive **FREE** books, daily deals, and stay current with news about upcoming releases and our hottest authors.
Scan the QR code below to sign up.

Already a subscriber? Please accept a sincere thank you for being a fan of Black Rose Writing authors.

View other Black Rose Writing titles at
www.blackrosewriting.com/books and use promo code
PRINT to receive a **20% discount** when purchasing.

CPSIA information can be obtained
at www.ICGtesting.com
Printed in the USA
LVHW031254020223
738347LV00004B/11

9 781685 130954